THE ADVENTURE GUIDE TO PUERTO RICO

Harry S. Pariser

MPC
HUNTER
PUBLISHING INC

Hunter Publishing, Inc.
300 Raritan Center Parkway
Edison NJ 08818
(201) 225 1900

ISBN 1–55650–178–1

Printed in Singapore through Palace Press

Published in the UK by:
Moorland Publishing Co. Ltd.
Moor Farm Road, Airfield Estate
Ashbourne, Derbyshire DE6 1HD
England

ISBN (UK) 086190–315–3

Photo Credits
Meredith Pillon, Puerto Rico Tourism Co.: 7, 38, 42, 86, 88, 120,
132, 137, 154, 174, 180, 190, 191. Jarma Mattila, P.R.T. Co.: 6, 152,
156. Margo Taussig Pinkerton: viii, 29, 134, 140, 142. P.R.T. Co.:
159. Cornell University: 185. All others by Harry S. Pariser.
Coqui drawing by Jennifer Ewing.

CONTENTS

iv   Contents

ABOUT THE AUTHOR

Harry S. Pariser was born in Pittsburgh and grew up in a small town in southwestern Pennsylvania. After graduating from Boston University with a B.S. in Public Communications in 1975, Harry hitched and camped his way through Europe, traveled down the Nile by steamer, and by train through Sudan. After visiting Uganda, Rwanda, and Tanzania, he traveled by passenger ship from Mombasa to Bombay, and then on through South and Southeast Asia before settling down in Kyoto, Japan, where he studied Japanese and ceramics while supporting himself by teaching English to everyone from tiny tots to Buddhist priests. Using Japan as a base, he returned to other parts of Asia: trekking to the vicinity of Mt. Everest in Nepal, taking tramp steamers to remote Indonesian islands like Adonara, Timor, Sulawesi, and Ternate, and visiting rural areas in China. He returned to the United States in 1984 from Kanazawa, Japan, via the Caribbean where he did research for two travel guides: Guide to Jamaica and Guide to Puerto Rico and the Virgin Islands, the first editions of which were published in 1986. Returning to Japan in 1986, he lived in the city of Kagoshima—a city at the southern tip of Kyushu which lies across the bay from an active volcano. During that year and part of the next, he taught English and wrote numerous articles for *The Japan Times*. He currently lives in San Francisco. Besides traveling and writing, his other pursuits include printmaking, painting, cooking, hiking, photography, reading, and listening to music—especially jazz.

ACKNOWLEDGMENTS

Many thanks to my publisher Michael Hunter and his staff. Thanks also go out to Prof. Juan Rafael Palmer, John Santos (music), the Crawfords, Lance Bon, Luis Torres, and David Minor (computer assistance).

HELP US KEEP THIS GUIDE UP-TO-DATE

In today's world, things change so rapidly that it's impossible for one person to keep up with everything happening in any one place. This is particularly true in the Caribbean, where situations are always in flux. Travel books are like automobiles: they require fine tuning and frequent overhauls to keep in shape. Help us keep this book in shape! We require input from our readers so that we can continue to provide the best, most current information available. Please write to let us know about any inaccuracies, new information, or misleading suggestions. Although we try to make our maps as accurate as possible, errors do occur. If you have any suggestions for improvement or places that should be included, please let us know about it.

We especially appreciate letters from female travelers, visiting expatriates, local residents, and hikers and outdoor enthusiasts. We also like hearing from experts in the field as well as from local hotel owners and individuals wishing to accommodate visitors from abroad.

INTRODUCTION

Despite the fact that Puerto Rico has been part of the territorial United States since 1898, most Americans know little or nothing about the island. Yet, Puerto Rico is perhaps the most exotic place in the country—a miniature Latin America set in the Caribbean. It is also one of the oldest locations in the territorial U.S.: San Juan was a thriving town while Jamestown was still an undeveloped plot of land. A very attractive island, Puerto Rico contains numerous forest reserves, beaches, ancient Indian sites, an abundance of historical atmosphere, and the only tropical National Forest in the U.S. Sadly, the vast majority of visitors get stuck in the tourist traps of Condado and never experience the island's charms.

THE LAND

the big picture: The islands of the Caribbean extend in a 2,800-mile (4,500-km) arc from the western tip of Cuba to the small Dutch island of Aruba. The region is sometimes extended to include the Central and S. American countries of Belize (the former colony of British Honduras), the Yucatan, Surinam, Guiana, and Guyana. The islands of Jamaica, Hispaniola, Puerto Rico, the U.S. and British Virgin Islands, along with Cuba, the Cayman, Turks, and Caicos islands form the Greater Antilles. The name derives from the early geographers, who gave the name "Antilia" to hypothetical islands thought to lie beyond the no less imaginary "Antilades." In

Culebra

general, the land is steep and volcanic in origin: chains of mountains run across Jamaica, Cuba, Hispaniola, and Puerto Rico, and hills rise abruptly from the sea along most of the Virgin Islands.

geography: Smallest and most easterly of the Greater Antilles, Puerto Rico's 3,435 sq miles (8,768 sq km—roughly the size of Connecticut, Crete, or Corsica) serve as one of the barriers between Caribbean and the Atlantic waters: the N coast faces the Atlantic while the E and S coasts face the Caribbean. The Virgin Islands lie to the E; to the W the 75-mile-wide (121-km) Mona Passage separates the island from neighboring Hispaniola. The seas off the coast are peppered with numerous cays and some small islands. The small archipelago of Culebra and the island of Vieques lie off the E coast while the even smaller Mona lies to the W. An irregular submarine shelf, seven miles at its widest, surrounds the island. Two miles off the N coast the sea floor plummets to 6,000 ft. (1,829 m); the Milwaukee Deep, which at 28,000 ft. (8,534 m) is one of the world's deepest underwater chasms, lies 45 miles (72 km) to the N. The nearly rectangular island runs 111 miles (179 km) from E to W and 36 miles (58 km) from N to S. Numerous headlands and indentations punctuate its coastline. Volcanic in origin, Puerto Rico is the tip of a huge volcanic mass. The coastal plain, an elevated area of land which rings the island, encircles the mountainous center. Two mountain ranges, the Luquillo and the Cordillera Central, cross the island from E to W. The Sierra de Luquillo in the E contains El Yunque ("The Anvil"), which reaches 3,843 ft. (1,171 m). A smaller range, the Sierra de Cayey, is in the SE. Cordillera Central, a broader *sierra* to the W, contains Cerro De Punta, which at 4,398 ft. (1,319 m) is the highest peak on the island. Spectacular shapes along the NW of the island are the result of karstification—a process whereby, over a million-year period, heavy rains seeping through the primary structural lines and joints of the porous limestone terrain carved huge caves, deep sinkholes, and long underground passages. As a result, the island is honeycombed with caves, the most famous located near Aguas Buenas. There are a total of 57 rivers and 1,200 streams on the island. Commercially valuable minerals include iron, manga-

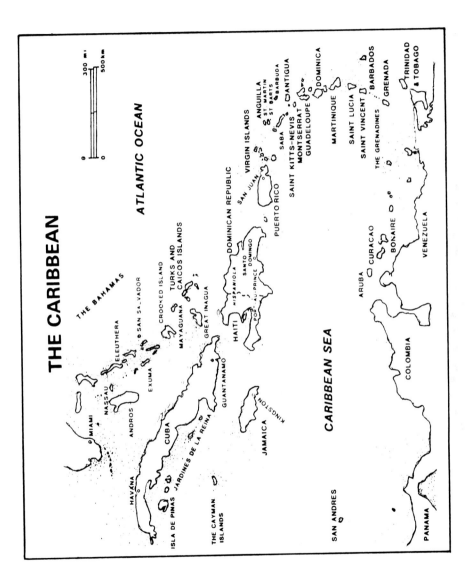

THE CARIBBEAN

nese, coal, marble, gypsum, clay, kaolin, phosphate, salt, and copper.

Climate

With an average temperature of 73°F during the coolest month and 79°F during the warmest, the island has a delightful climate. Located within the belt of the steady NE trade winds, its mild, subtropical climate varies little throughout the year. Winter temperatures average 19° warmer than Cairo and Los Angeles, seven degrees warmer than Miami, and four degrees warmer than Honolulu. Temperatures in the mountain areas average eight to 10 degrees cooler than on the coast. Lowest recorded temperature (40°F) was measured at Aibonito in March, 1911. Only five days per year are entirely without sunshine. Rain, which usually consists of short showers, is most likely to occur between June and October. The N coast receives much more rain than the S, with San Juan receiving 60 in. per year as compared with Ponce's 30. Trade winds produce the greatest amount of rain in the mountain areas, with El Yunque averaging 183 in. (4648 mm) per year, which falls in some 1,600 showers.

hurricanes: Cast in a starring role as the bane of the tropics, hurricanes represent the one outstanding negative in an otherwise impeccably hospitable climate. The Caribbean as a whole ranks third worldwide in the number of hurricanes per year. These low-pressure zones are serious business and should not be taken lightly. Where the majority of structures are held together only by nails and rope, a hurricane is no joke and property damaged from them may run into the hundreds of millions of dollars. A hurricane begins as a relatively small tropical storm, known as a cyclone when its winds reach a velocity of 39 mph (62 kph). At 74 mph (118 kph) it is upgraded to hurricane status, with winds up to 200 mph (320 kph) and ranging in size from 60–1,000 miles (100–1,600 km) in diameter. A small hurricane releases energy equivalent to the explo-

PUERTO RICO CLIMATE CHART

	Daily Average Air Temp. °F	Rainfall Days	Rainfall Inches
January	80	20	4.3
February	80	15	2.7
March	81	15	2.9
April	82	14	4.1
May	84	16	5.9
June	85	17	5.4
July	85	19	5.7
August	85	20	6.3
September	86	18	6.2
October	85	18	5.6
November	84	19	6.3
December	81	21	5.4

sions of six atomic bombs per second. A hurricane may be compared to an enormous hovering engine that uses the moist air and water of the tropics as fuel, carried hither and thither by prevailing air currents—generally eastern trade winds which intensify as they move across warm ocean waters. When cooler, drier air infiltrates it as it heads N, the hurricane begins to die, cut off from the life-sustaining ocean currents that have nourished it from infancy. Routes and patterns are unpredictable. As for their frequency: "June—too soon; July—stand by; August—it must; September—remember." So goes the old rhyme. Unfortunately, hurricanes are not confined to July and August. Hurricanes forming in Aug. and Sept. typically last for two weeks while those that form in June, July, Oct., and Nov. (many of which originate in the Caribbean and the Gulf of Mexico) generally last only seven days. Approximately 70% of all hurricanes (known as Cabo Verde types) originate as embryonic storms coming from the W coast of Africa. Fortunately though, they are comparatively scarce in the area around Puerto Rico. Since record-keeping began in 1508, 73 hurricanes have wreaked havoc on the island. The most serious of these have been San Felipe and San Ciprian, which hit in 1928 and 1932. The most recent hurricane to visit Puerto Rico was Santa Clara, on 12 Aug., 1956.

Flamboyant tree

Flora

Puerto Rico's central location in the northern Caribbean, together with its variations in elevation, rainfall, and soil, have
served to stimulate the development of a varied plant life.
These variations account for five differing areas of natural

vegetation: humid sea forest or marshland; humid wood forest; the humid tropical forest found in the center of the island; the subhumid forest along the NW coast; and the thorny dry forest on the S coast. Although 75% of the island was covered by forest a century ago, today it's only 25%, with a bare 1% of the forest retaining its virginity. Natural ground cover can be found in El Yunque Park and the forest reserves of Puerto Rico. Although a considerable number of the 3,355 species of flora are indigenous, many have been introduced from neighboring islands. Native trees include the *ceiba*, or silk cotton tree; famous for its enormous size, it may live 300 years or more. Masks and eating utensils have traditionally been made from the gourd of the *higuero* or calabash tree. The unopened leaves of the Puerto Rican hat palm are still put to use in weaving fine hats and baskets, but the *ausobo*, a type of ironwood used for ceiling beams during the colonial era, has virtually disappeared. Imported trees include the Australian casuarina, the cassia, the Mexican *papayuelo*, the Indo-

View from Parador Hacienda Gripinas near Jayuya

Malayan coconut palm, the mango, and the tamarind. Altogether, there are 547 native species of trees, with an additional 203 naturalized species—an incredible variety for such a small area. Ornamental vines and shrubs include bougainvillea, *carallita*, jasmine, hibiscus, shower of orchids, gardenia, thunbergia, poinsettia, and croton.

Fauna

Except for bats, dolphins, and sea cows (manatee), Puerto Rico has no indigenous mammals. One extinct species is the multicolored mute dog which the Indians liked to fatten up and roast. Cows, pigs, mongooses, and horses were all imported by the Spanish. Although there was once a great demand in the Spanish Antilles for Puerto Rican horses and cattle, this industry has almost died out. *Paso fino* and *anadura* horses are still held in popular esteem; the former can walk at a pace which enables a rider to carry a full glass of water in his hand and not spill a drop. Mongooses, imported from India to combat rats and now-extinct poisonous reptiles, have propagated to the point where they too have now become an agricultural pest.

birdlife: There are approximately 200 species of birds including the Puerto Rican grackle, the kingbird, the petchary, several species of owls, and the Puerto Rican sharp-shinned and West Indian red-tailed hawks. Once a million strong, the colorful Puerto Rican parrot has dwindled to numbers bordering extinction and now resides only in the outback areas of El Yunque. Among the smaller birds are the onomatopoetically named *pitirre,* and the *reinita* ("little queen") which hangs out around kitchen windows and tables.

reptiles and amphibians: If Puerto Rico can be said to have a national animal, it must be the diminutive *coquí.* This one-and-a-half inch (36 mm) streamlined treefrog features bulging eyes, webbed fingers and toes with 10 highly efficient suction discs, and smooth, nearly transparent beige skin. Its cry is enchanting, so sweet that it's sometimes mistaken by new-

Coqui

comers for that of a bird. Once thought to be only a single species, it actually comes in 16 varieties. Its evening concert has won it a special place in the hearts of Puerto Ricans all across the island. A rather different type of animal is the protected gigantic tortoise which is closely related to its more famous cousins on the Galapagos. Culebra's population of giant leatherback turtles, which come ashore to lay their eggs, is on the verge of extinction.

insects and spiders: A full 15,000 species of insects include a vast variety ranging from the lowly cockroach to 216 species of butterflies and moths. *Mimes* are tiny, biting sand flies. The local tarantula, the *guaba*, is one of about 10 spiders on the island. Another is the *arana bobo* or "silly spider." The bite of the centipede, which grows up to 15 in. (38 cm) long, will prove traumatic if not fatal.

fish and marinelife: Species of fish include the leather jacket, sawfish, parrotfish, weakfish, lionfish, big-eye fish, bananafish, ladyfish, puffer, sea-bat, sardine, mullet, grouper, Spanish and frigate mackerels, red snapper, eel, barracuda, and a variety of sharks. While swimming, beware of stings from jellyfish, called *agua viva* or "living water," and avoid trampling on that armed knight of the underwater sand dunes, the sea urchin. Hard- and soft-shelled crabs include the *cangrejo, buruquena, juey,* and *jaiba.*

coral reefs: Indisputably the most important living organisms in the island's history, corals produce the calcium carbonate responsible for the buildup of most of the island's offlying cays and islets as well as most of the sand on the beaches. Bearing the brunt of waves, they also conserve the shoreline.

Aerial view of Culebra

Although reefs were formed milleniums ago, they are in a constant state of flux. Seemingly solid, they actually depend upon a delicate ecological balance to survive. Deforestation, dredging, temperature change, an increase or decrease in salinity, or sewage discharge may kill them. Because temperature ranges must remain between 68° and 95°, they are only found in the tropics. Acting more like plants than animals, they survive through photosynthesis: the algae inside the coral polyps do the work while the polyps themselves secrete calcium carbonate and stick together for protection from waves and boring sponges. Reefs originate as the polyps die, forming a base for the next generation.

Puerto Rican reefs: Most common are fringing reefs which occur close to shore, perhaps separated by a small lagoon. Elongated and narrow bank or ribbon reefs are offshore in deep water. Atolls and barrier reefs are absent. Fringing reefs exist at Seven Seas Beach in Las Croabas, Fajardo and along several other offshore cays in the NE corner of the island; at Guayama and Salinas; near Caja de Muertos Island off the coast from Ponce; at La Parguera; and off the coast of Mona Island. Bank reefs exist near Culebra and Vieques.

HISTORY

pre-European habitation: Believed to have arrived anywhere between 5 and 20,000 years ago on rafts from Florida via Cuba, the Arcaicos or Archaics—food gatherers and fisherman—were the first settlers. Little evidence of their habitation survives. Believed to have reached the island perhaps as early as 200 B.C., the Igneri, a sub-group of Northern South American's Arawaks, were agriculturists who brought tobacco and corn with them. Last to appear and most culturally advanced, the Tainos arrived from the S between AD 1,000 and 1,500; these copper-skinned, dark haired people were expert carvers (in shell, gold, stone, wood, and clay) and skilled agriculturalists, cultivating cassava, corn, beans, and squash. They gave the island the name of Boriquen—"Land of the Noble Lord," after the creator Yukiyu who was believed to reside in the heart of the present-day Caribbean National Forest.

European discovery: During his second voyage in 1493, Columbus stopped off at the island of Santa Maria de Guadalupe. Here, he met 12 Taino women and two young boys who said that they wished to return to their home on the island of Boriquen (Puerto Rico). Columbus took the Indians along with him as guides. On 19 Nov., the Indians, spying their home island, leapt into the water and swam ashore. Columbus named the island San Juan Bautista ("Saint John the Baptist") after the Spanish Prince Don Juan. The island was colonized under the leadership of Juan Ponce de Leon in 1508, and he was appointed governor in 1509. Soon, Franciscan friars arrived with cattle and horses; a gold smelter was set up and production begun. On 8 Nov., 1511, this first settlement was renamed Puerto Rico ("Rich Port") and a coat of arms was granted. King Ferdinand distributed the island's land and the 30,000 Tainos among the soldiers. Under the system of *repartimiento* ("distribution") Indians were accosted and set to work in con-

IMPORTANT DATES IN PUERTO RICAN HISTORY

1493: 19 November, Columbus "discovers" the island of Puerto Rico on his second voyage, naming it San Juan Bautista.

1508: Juan Ponce de Leon is appointed governor and founds Caparra, the first settlement.

1509: Government seat is moved and named Ciudad de Puerto Rico.

1521: The capital is renamed San Juan while the entire island takes the name Puerto Rico.

1530: Having exhausted the gold supply, many colonists migrate to Peru in search of new plunder while those remaining become farmers.

1595: Sir Francis Drake unsuccessfully attacks San Juan.

1598: The Count of Cumberland, capturing San Juan, holds it for seven months.

1625: 24 September, attack by a Dutch fleet is repelled but not before its troops sack the city.

1631: Construction begins on El Morro.

1680: Ponce is founded.

1760: Mayaguez is founded.

1775: Population reaches 70,000, including 6,467 slaves.

1778: Private ownership of land is granted by the Crown.

1790: British attack and pull out after a one-month siege.

1800: Island population estimated at 155,406.

1821: First of a series of 19th C. slave rebellions takes place in Bayamon.

1822–1837: Tyrannical rule of Governor Miguel de la Torre, Spanish Commander defeated by Bolivar in Venezuela in 1821.

1833: Blacks forbidden to serve in the military.

1859: Patriot and leader Luis Munoz Rivera born.

1860: Population reaches 583,308.

1868: The famous *Grito de Lares* revolt occurs.

1873: Abolition of slavery.

1891: *Independista* leader Pedro Albizu Campos is born.

1897: 25 November, autonomy granted by Spain.

1898: 25 July, American troops land at Guanica and establish control.

1899: 11 April, Spain cedes Puerto Rico to the U.S. under the Treaty of Paris.

1900: Under the Foraker Act, Puerto Rico becomes a U.S. territory; an American-led civil administration replaces the military.

1917: 2 March, the Jones Act makes Puerto Ricans U.S. citizens.

1937: 12 March, the "Ponce Massacre" occurs when police fire on an *Independista* parade, killing 19 and injuring 100.

1938: Attempted assassination of Gov. Winship.

1942: Tugwell, last U.S. governor, appointed.

1950: Public Law 600 permits Puerto Rico to draft constitution. *Independistas* attack La Fortaleza; riots result. Attempted assassination of Truman on 1 Nov.; wounding five Congressmen. Campos and others jailed.

1965: Abolishment of literacy tests under the Civil Rights Act.

1967: Commonwealth status wins approval by 60.5 percent in a referendum.

1972: Roberto Clemente, Pittsburgh Pirate and island hero, dies in a plane crash while on relief mission to earthquake-struck Managua, Nicaragua.

1973: Bishop of San Juan, Luis Aponte Martinez, appointed Cardinal by Pope Paul VI.

---

struction and in the mines or fields. Under a similar system, termed *ecomienda* ("commandery"), they were forcibly extracted from villages and set to labor for a *patron* on his estate. Although, in return, the Indians were supposed to receive protection and learn about the wonders of Catholicism, this system was a thinly disguised form of slavery which ultimately led to the extinction of the native inhabitants as a distinct racial and cultural group. The Indians tragically assumed that these newcomers, owing to their remarkable appearance and superior technology, were immortal. A chieftain decided to put this theory to the test, and a young Spaniard, Diego Salcedo, was experimentally drowned while being carried across the Rio Grande de Anasco in the NW part of the island. When he did not revive after three days, the Indians realized their mistake, then killed nearly half the Spaniards on the island. The revolt was put down, however, and many Indians fled to the mountains or neighboring islands. Most of the Indians were freed by royal decrees in 1521, but it was too late: they'd already been absorbed into the racial fabric. With the depletion of both Indians and gold, a new profit making scheme had to be found. That proved to be the new "gold" of the Caribbean:

Landscape, Vieques

sugar. The first sugar mill was built in 1523 near Anasco, and the entire economy changed from mining to sugar over the next few decades. The first Portuguese slavers, filled to the brim with captive Africans intended to provide agricultural labor, arrived in 1518. The city of Puerto Rico was moved to the site of present-day San Juan, which name it took, and the entire island in turn was renamed Puerto Rico. Puerto Rico became one of Spain's strategic outposts in the Caribbean; ignoring the economic potential of the island, hardnosed military commanders appointed by Madrid treated the island as if it were one huge military installation. An attack by Sir Francis Drake's fleet in 1595 was repelled, but the English Count of Cumberland launched a successful invasion in 1598. Harsh natural elements, coupled with the effects of dysentery, caused him and his troops to exit shortly thereafter. The Dutch besieged San Juan in 1625; defeated, they did succeed in torching a great deal of the city. Forbidden to trade except within the Spanish Empire, Puerto Rico developed a brisk interisland business in contraband goods (ginger, tobacco, and cattle hides) during the mid-16th century. In April 1797, the British, under the command of Abercrombie, led an unsuccessful attack against San Juan.

the nineteenth century: The Puerto Rican political scene was divided into loyalists, liberals, and separatists. In March, 1812 a new constitution, more liberal than the previous one, was approved for Puerto Rico, and Puerto Ricans became Spanish citizens. With the arrival of Canary Islanders, Haitians, Louisiana French, Venezuelans, and black slaves, Puerto Rico became a lively potpourri of cultures. As the population exploded, a new nationalism—a distinct sense of being Puerto Rican—began to emerge. From 1825–67 the island was governed by a series of ruthless, despotic military commanders known as the "Little Caesars." During the 1850s, Ramon Emeterio Betances became the leader of the separatist movement and founded the Puerto Rican Revolutionary Movement in Santo Domingo. At midnight on 23 Sept., 1868, several hundred rebels marched into and took over the town of Lares. Hearing news of the revolt, the government placed reinforcements at nearby San Sebastian, and the rebels took to the hills. A guerrilla war ensued and lasted a month. This was the famous *Grito de Lares* ("The Cry of Lares"). Even though this first (and only) attempt at rebellion failed, it is cited by *independentistas* as a major event in Puerto Rican history. In 1869, Puerto Rico sent its first representatives to the Cortes, the Spanish House of Representatives. A law abolishing slavery became effective on 22 March, 1873, though "freed" slaves had to continue toiling for their masters for another three years as indentured laborers; full civil rights were granted five years later. Led by Luis Munoz Riviera, the Autonomous Party was formed in 1882. On 28 Nov., 1897, Prime Minister Sagasta signed a royal decree establishing "autonomy" for Puerto Rico, though on paper only. Included in the package was voting representation in the two houses of the Spanish Cortes (legislature).

American annexation: In the furor (spurred on by American newspaper barons Hearst and Pulitzer) following the explosion of the battleship *Maine* on 15 February, 1898, President McKinley declared war with Spain. In July, just as the new government had begun to function, Gen. Nelson A. Miles landed on the island at Guanica with 16,000 U.S. troops. The Puerto Rican campaign of the Spanish-American War lasted only 17 days and was described by one journalist as a "picnic." On 10 Dec. 1898, under the Treaty of Paris accords signed by the United States and Spain, Puerto Rico was ceded to the U.S. With no consultation whatsoever, the Puerto Ricans overnight found themselves under American rule after nearly 400 years of Spanish occupation. Intellectuals on the island had high expectations from the U.S. government; after all, Gen. Miles had promised "to give the people of your beautiful island the largest measure of liberty (and) to bestow upon you . . . the liberal institutions of our government." Naturally, this meant attempting to make the Puerto Ricans as "American" as possible up to and including changing the name to "Porto" Rico—in order to make it easy to spell! Hopes for independence were dashed, however, as two years of military rule were followed by the Foraker Act. In effect from 1900–16, the act placed Puerto Rico in an ambiguous purgatory in which the government was a mix of autocracy and democracy. Americanization continued by importing teachers who taught classes entirely in English—an unsuccessful tactic. Requests by island leaders for a plebiscite to determine the island's status were ignored. In 1909, enraged by the provisions of the Foraker Act, the Puerto Rican House of Delegates refused to pass any legislation at all. This protest brought no change in status, and by the beginning of WW I, there was widespread talk of independence.

citizenship: In order to secure Puerto Rico as both a strategic defense bastion and a ready supply of "raw materials" for the slaughter mills of Europe, Puerto Ricans were granted American citizenship by the Jones-Shafroth Act. Under this bill, which President Woodrow Wilson signed into law on 2 March 1917, Puerto Ricans automatically became U.S. citizens unless they signed a statement rejecting it. If they refused, they stood to lose a number of civil rights, including the right to hold office, and would then have received alien status! Naturally, only a few refused. Another request two years later for a plebiscite also failed. In 1922, local politician Antonio Barcelo tried a new approach: he proposed an association which would be modeled after the Irish Free State; the bill died in committee. The same year marked the formation of the Nationalist Party.

the 1930s depression: High unemployment, political anarchy, and near starvation reigned as the depression years of the 1930s hit Puerto Rico even harder than the mainland. Pedro Albizu Campos, a Harvard Law School Graduate and former U.S. Army officer, emerged as head of the new Nationalist Party. After members of the party turned to violence, followed in turn by police brutality and oppression, Campos and seven of his followers found themselves in jail in Atlanta, Georgia. On 21 March 1936, after a permit to hold a Palm Sunday parade was revoked by the government at the last moment, Nationalists went ahead with it anyway. As *La Bouriquena* played in the background, police opened fire on protestors, innocent bystanders, and fellow policemen. This event, known as *La Masacre de Ponce,* resulted in the deaths of 20 and the wounding of 100 persons.

commonwealth status: Luiz Munoz Marin, son of Luis Munoz Rivera, and his Popular Democratic Party came to power in 1940 with a 37% plurality. Perhaps the dominant figure in all of Puerto Rican history, Munoz presided over the governmental, economic, and educational transformation of the island. He served for eight years as Senate majority leader before becoming the island's first elected governor in 1948. After his election he changed from being pro-independence to pro-commonwealth. On 30 Oct. 1950, there were *independentista* uprisings on the island. That same week, *independentistas* opened fire outside Blair House, President Truman's temporary abode in Washington, D.C. Resistance leader Pedro Albizu-Campos was charged with inciting armed insurrection and imprisoned. On 4 June 1951, Puerto Ricans approved a referendum granting commonwealth status to Puerto Rico. As the only other alternative was continued colonial status, many Puerto Ricans failed to show up at the ballot box. In a second referendum the new constitution was approved, and commonwealth status (*Estado Libre Asociado* or "free associated state") was inaugurated on 25 July 1952. While the new status superficially resembled that of a state of the Union, Puerto Ricans still paid no income tax and were forbidden to vote in national elections or elect voting representatives to Congress. In 1954, two Puerto Ricans (New York City residents) wounded five Congressmen when they opened fire in the House of Representatives in Washington. In 1964, Munoz stepped down, and Roberto Sanchez Vilella became the island's second elected governor. A plebiscite sponsored by the *Populares* was held on 23 July 1967, although the statehooder Luis A. Ferre and *Independentista* Hector Alvarez Silver bolted to form their own parties. The buoyant economy, coupled with strong support for commonwealth status by the ever-influential Munoz, caused a record turnout (with 65.9% of the eligible voters participating) in which 60% of the voters supported commonwealth status, 39% supported statehood, and .06% supported independence. In 1968, Luis A. Ferre, head of the newly created New Progressive Party, was elected governor, and he began to push actively for statehood. On 26 Sept. 1969, when an *independentista* was jailed for one year for draft evasion, col-

Trolley, Old San Juan

lege students set fire to the ROTC building at Rio Piedras. In the aftermath, seven students were suspended and marches and counter marches degenerated into riots. Polarization between the various political elements continues to this day.

GOVERNMENT

There is possibly no other island of its size where politics is as hot an issue as it is in Puerto Rico. In spite of the fact that elections determine nothing save who will deliver what slice of the political patronage, Puerto Ricans eat, drink, sleep, and breathe politics. Some even consider politics to be Puerto Rico's national sport. In addition, Puerto Rico has one of the most curious political systems in the world. Although it's a colony of the U.S., the island has commonwealth rather than colonial status. Puerto Ricans have U.S. citizenship and freedom of travel to and from the States. Yet, although Puerto Ricans may be drafted, they may not vote in U.S. elections. Undoubtedly, the ambivalence of Puerto Rico's status is unequaled anywhere in the world.

administrative organization: It is divided into executive, legislative, and judicial branches just as on the mainland. Governors are elected for a four-year term. The executive branch is extremely powerful and governors appoint more than 500 executive and judicial branch officials. The bicameral legislature consists of a 27-member *Senado* (Senate) and a 51-member *Camara de Representantes* (House of Representatives). In order to prevent one party from dominating the legislature, both houses may be increased by additional minority party members when any one party gains more than two-thirds of the seats in an election. In this situation, the number of seats may be increased up to a maximum of nine in the *Senado* and 17 in the *Camara*. These "at large" seats are apportioned among party members according to the electoral strength of each minority party. Spanish is the language used in both houses, as well as throughout the courts. Puerto Rico's Supreme Court heads the unified judicial system. Contested decisions made by the Court may be reviewed by the U.S. Supreme Court. Puerto Rico is also part of the Federal District Court System. Instead of being divided into counties, Puerto Rico is sectioned into 78 municipalities, many of them mere villages. Each has a mayor and municipal assembly elected every four years. Technically a congressman, Puerto Rico's non-voting Resident Commissioner sits in the U.S. House of Representatives in Washington, D.C. Unlike other congressmen, he is elected only once every four years and represents a constituency seven times as large as the average.

the question of status: The single most important and hotly debated issue in Puerto Rico centers on the issue of political status. There are three distinct possibilities for Puerto Rico's future status. One would be the continuation of the present commonwealth status in its current or modified form. The second is statehood. The third and least likely would be independence. Modification of the commonwealth status would involve granting more autonomy to the island government while retaining ties with the U.S. Autonomy would be granted over trade tariffs, immigration, the minimum wage, and federal grants, and would be coupled with exemption from ICC and FCC regulations. Elevation to statehood, on the other hand, would require a severe economic transition. Chase Manhattan and Citibank, which provide most of the island's financing, would find themselves in violation of interstate banking regulations and would have to close their operations there. Income tax, now paid only to the local government, would have to be turned over to the federal government. Statehood would also mean forfeiture of tax-exempt status for Puerto Rico's industries. Support for statehood is growing, not because the islanders have an explicit wish to enter the American mainstream, but because the politicians are selling the story that it will bring increased revenues and more money. The coconut palm is the symbol of the New Progressive Party and its leaders assure followers that *los cocos* (dollars) will rain down on them after statehood is achieved. However, there is little incentive for the U.S. Congress to grant Puerto Rico statehood status. Statehood is also controversial not only because most Puerto Ricans cannot speak English fluently, but also because Puerto Rico's large population and high birth rate would give it more congressional representatives than 20 other states. Independence, the third and least likely alternative, is supported by a small but vocal minority. There has long been serious talk of independence in Puerto Rico, but as things stand now popular support is lacking. One reason is that Puerto Ricans fear the political and economic chaos that independence might bring. The independence movement in Puerto Rico has a long tradition of using terrorist tactics, which has resulted in official government repression. Recent attacks include the Nov. 1979 ambush of a U.S. army bus on the island in which two were killed and three wounded. The island is of such strategic military importance and is so economically tied to the U.S. that a meaningful change in status is unlikely under the prevailing political and economic conditions.

political parties: If Puerto Rico's political status seems confusing, so are the vast number and varied politics of its many partidos (parties), some of which hardly engender enough support to be worthy of the name. There is no dominant party in Puerto Rican politics; instead, there are a number of factions, none of which ever receives majority support. The two major political parties are the *Partido Popular Democratica* (Popular Democratic Party or PPD), headed by Governor Rafael Hernandez Colon, and the *Partido Progressiva Nueva* (New Progressive Party or PPN), led by Carlos Romero Barcelo. Each has a half a million hardcore supporters, out of a total two million registered voters. The Popular Democratic Party supports continued maintenance of commonwealth status provided it is revised to allow more autonomy. The PPN's Carlos Romero Barcelo, nicknamed *El Cabrallo* ("the horse") by his detractors because he is allegedly stubborn, ruthless, and macho, served as governor from 1976–84. His party supports statehood for the island, but because Americanization is seen as a prerequisite, he and his party, whose members are dubbed *"estadistas"* ("statehooders"), are frequently regarded as enemies of Puerto Rican culture. Former San Juan Mayor Hernan Padilla's Puerto Rican Renewal Party is a PPN splinter party with 300,000 supporters. There are also two independence parties; the larger is the socialistic Puerto Rican Independence Party, formed in 1946 and led by Ruben Berrios-Martinez. The Puerto Rican Socialist Party, founded in 1946 and led by Juan Mari-Bras, advocates independence by any means. Bubbling below the surface are the *Fuerzas Armadas de Liberacion Nacional* (FALN) and the *Macheteros*. While the FALN terrorizes targets on the mainland, the *Macheteros* now confine themselves to such island targets as the San Juan Power Station and Fort Buchanan. They claim responsibility for the 12 Sept. 1983 robbery of the Wells Fargo terminal in West Hartford, Connecticut, which netted $7 million—the second largest heist in U.S. history.

recent political history: Carlos Romero Barcelo of the New Progressive Party won the governorship over the Popular Democratic Party's Hernandez Colon by 43,000 votes in 1976 and by a 3,000-vote margin in 1980. After the polls closed in 1980, Commandant Enrique Sanchez, security chief in charge of polling and a Romero henchman, refused for hours to turn over the ballots to the counting authorities. What happened to the ballots in that time remains a mystery. On 25 July 1978 security forces shot and killed two *independentistas* atop Cerro Maravilla, Puerto Rico's highest peak, which is topped with communications towers. Apparently, two youths, Arnaldo Dario Posado and Carlos Soto Arrivi, were lured by undercover agent Gonzalez Malaveto to the mountaintop to plant explosives. It is believed that the youths, one mentally disturbed and the other a teenager, were enticed there and then shot in order to discredit the independence movement. Though no one will ever know the exact truth, the official government story has been thoroughly discredited. In addition, seven former police officers involved in the case have since been sentenced to 20–30 years each on charges of perjury and obstructing justice. Three officers remain to be tried for first-degree murder for their involvement in the slayings. And disclosure of possible involvement by members of his administration or by Romero himself in the entrapment at Cerro Maravilla was a major contributing factor in his 1984 defeat to the PDP's Rafael Hernandez Colon. The first primary gubernatorial contests held in the island's history were in June 1988 between San Juan Mayor Balthasar Corrada del Rio and Romero Barcelo. Corrada won but went on to lose the November 1988 election to Hernandez Colon.

ECONOMY

Much is made of the economic "miracle" which is taking place in Puerto Rico. It's true that in 1983 Puerto Rico's GNP reached $13 billion; not only is this the Caribbean's highest, but it is almost $2 billion above Cuba's, though that country

Old San Juan doorway

has a much larger area and three times the population. Per capita income for 1983 was $3,900, highest in the Caribbean after the U.S. Virgin Islands. Yet, Puerto Rico's economy is troubled. Now totally interdependent with the U.S., the entire economic structure had undergone a thorough transformation since the U.S. invasion in 1898. At that time Puerto Rico was a subsistence-level agricultural society largely dependent upon crops like sugar, coffee, and tobacco. While these are still of some importance to the economy, the overriding emphasis today is on manufacturing, with tourism coming second.

American involvement: The history of the Puerto Rican economy is the story of the U.S. economic presence in Latin America rendered in microcosm. After cession by Spain, the U.S. financial barons deemed the coffee crop, once the major generator of income, unprofitable. Devastated by the 1899 hurricane, coffee farmers were refused a loan by the Executive Council set up by the Americans to rule the island. As a consequence, the coffee economy was soon supplanted by sugar, and American companies were quick to establish themselves. By 1930, 60% of the banking and 80% of the tobacco industry were under the control of American interests, and by 1935, nearly 50% of all lands operated by sugar companies were under the control of four big American concerns. Although a law limited farms to 500 acres, these giants had an average of 40,000 acres each under their control. This trend has continued to the point where the small cane farmer has virtually disappeared, replaced by the large sugar corporations like those of the Serralles family empire. The 1930's depression period hit Puerto Rico extremely hard and resulted in the decline of the sugar, needlework, and tobacco industries. At the end of WW II, less than 10% of Puerto Rico's workers held industrial jobs. In order to modernize the island and spur the sluggish economy, Fomento, the Economic Development Administration, was set up to attract industry—the island's 1950 hourly wage of 40¢ compared favorably with the $1.50 average wage stateside. A high rate of unemployment reduced the prospects for potential strikes.

Operation Bootstrap: By offering 10–30 year tax exemptions and low wages, this program has managed to lure 2,000 manufacturing plants to the island. Nearly 400 of these are operated by "Fortune 1,000" corporations. Needless to say, these companies are not here for altruistic reasons: they are here because, despite high power and shipping costs, tax incentives make the island a paradise for profitable investment. Under Section 936 of the IRS Code, American companies pay no federal taxes on profits earned in Puerto Rico. Although Congress acted in 1982 to slightly modify this section, U.S. companies still earned $2.8 billion in tax-free profits during 1982. The Treasury Department charges that the law has become a boondoggle, because it allows firms to reap huge profits while creating only a minimal amount of employment. Through a system known as "transfer pricing," corporations pay an inflated price for products purchased from their Puerto Rican subsidiaries, thus reducing their U.S.-gained profits on paper and their taxable income along with it. The Treasury estimates that 50% of the tax-exempt income in Puerto Rico in 1980 was generated by this and other such nefarious means— such as transferring ownership of patents and trademarks to the island. If 936 should ever be repealed, Puerto Rico Industrial Development Co. head Antonio Colorado estimates that 25–50% of all industrial firms will leave the island. In addition, the 21 companies which have planned to build "twin plants," which would link Puerto Rican plants with those in other Caribbean nations, have threatened to abandon their plans should the section be repealed. At present, total hourly labor costs on the island in manufacturing are half as high as in the States as a whole. Puerto Rico was intended to serve as a model to show what the miracle drug of capitalist investment can do for an undeveloped economy under the right circumstances. In these terms, Operation Bootstrap must be seen as a failure. Although U.S. investments in Puerto Rico are now the largest in all of Latin America (excluding Venezuela), the economy is in terrible shape: the economy has kept expanding, but employment has not. The explanation for this is very simple: capital intensive, rather than labor intensive, industries have been transplanted to Puerto Rico. For example, pharmaceutical companies do pay their workers more, but use relatively less labor.

manufacturing: Tax exemptions and other advantages have lured 24 pharmaceutical companies to the island; Puerto Rico produces 7% of the world's total supply of pharmaceuticals, and *all* of America's birth control pills. Figures for the year 1973 show that U.S. firms produced $500 million worth of drugs on the island. A Chase Manhattan study of the top seven firms showed that they saved more than $66 million because of their tax-exempt status; Lilly and Searle alone saved over $33 million that year. Besides saving on taxes, companies also avoid safety inspections: Puerto Rican men working in the birth control pill factories have begun to grow breasts after handling estrogen, some have even had radical mastectomies, and others have become impotent. In the States, this would cause an outrage, but in Puerto Rico it passes almost unnoticed. Manufacturing represents some 20% of total employment and generates $180 million in tax revenues, in addition to providing jobs in the construction, trade, and service industries. More than one-third of all manufacturing jobs are still in apparel and textiles. Many of these goods are destined for the States; the shoe industry ships 20 million pairs Stateside each year, and the island is the world's largest producer of rum. Excise taxes on each case of rum sold in the U.S. are rebated to Puerto Rico's Treasury. In 1982 this totaled $210 million, or 10% of the island's revenues. However, more than half of the molasses used in its manufacture and most rum is exported in bulk and bottled on the mainland in order to keep down costs. To produce all of these goods, Puerto Rico uses incredible amounts of electricity, most of it generated by imported oil, making the island more dependent on foreign oil than any of the 50 states. The island's homes and industries use twice as much energy as Hawaii, three times as much as Alaska, and nearly as much as the entire continent of Africa.

tourism: A growing sector, the tourism "industry" continues to increase its influence on the economy. Despite the tragic fire at the Dupont Plaza Hotel in Condado that claimed 96 lives on Dec. 31, 1986, hotel occupancy rates have continued to rise. More than $710 million was spent by visitors in 1985, accounting for 48,000 direct and indirect jobs and giving the government revenues amounting to $153 million. The average visitor

Condado

in 1986 spent $364 and the average hotel guest spent $627. In 1986, 448,529 people stayed in tourist hotels, 5,142 in guest houses, and 448,973 arrived by cruise ship. Another 1,118,919 also came, saw, and slept bringing the total number of visitors to 2,021,563. Guests at the tourist hotels were estimated to have spent $228,022,286; cruise ship passengers spent $23,101,658; and guest housers spent only a paltry $1,642,834.

mining: Although the original impetus for Spanish conquest of the island was gold, mining is no longer a major industry. Even though rich copper deposits have been discovered in the Lares-Utuado-Adjuntas area in the heart of the Cordillera Central, a drop in the world copper price, coupled with the determined opposition of environmentalists and *independentistas,* has so far kept the multinationals at bay.

prospects for the future: It is unlikely that Puerto Rico's economy will improve in the near future. Sixth largest customer of U.S. goods, Puerto Rico purchases some $4.5 billion annually in manufactured products from the States. This represents $3.5 billion in gross income for American business and workers, and employment for 200,000 Americans. This does not include, however, the profits stemming from transport of goods and people, from financial and banking transactions, and from insurance and advertising. In 1982, $4.1 billion in federal funds was sent to Puerto Rico: $2.4 billion for personal transfers (such as food stamps and Medicare), and the rest for functions such as immigration, customs, and the military, the island's single largest employer. Indeed, the relationship between Puerto Rico and the U.S. resembles the proverbial one between the worker and the company store. Instead of company bills of promise, the Puerto Ricans shop with *cupones*. Some $100 million in food stamps reach 53% of the populace and comprise 10% of the total distributed nationwide. Although Puerto Ricans pay more for food and the cost of living in general is higher, federal subsidies make life comfortable. Rather than having the Puerto Ricans themselves pay for these subsidies or taxing the companies who reap immense profits, the American taxpayer foots the bill! Currently, unemployment continues to rise. While the official figure is 20%, unofficial estimates are 30% or higher. Teen-age unemployment has soared to 60%. Including the men who have given up looking for work, the *ociosos voluntarios* (voluntary idle), there are more than 300,000 unemployed.

Agriculture

Like the economy in general, the agricultural situation in Puerto Rico has been in constant flux since the U.S. occupation in 1898. Sugarcane, once the backbone of the economy and still a major crop, has become an economic drain. The government buys most of the crop and operates its own sugar mills, but even with subsidies the $3.35 minimum wage dictates that the cost cannot compete with neighboring islands like the Dominican Republic, where labor is much cheaper. The government loses money on every pound of sugar, and this industry is little more than a costly, outmoded public employment program. Devastated by the 1899 and 1928 hurricanes, coffee production is now down to 26 million pounds per year. Once another flourishing crop, tobacco production continues to decline, and the largest processing plant shut its doors in 1977. The government neglect of agriculture in favor of industry since WW II has served to guarantee that local products are ignored in favor of expensive imports from the States. The percentage of farmers in the workforce has plummeted from 35 to 5%, and 80% of all food is imported. Imported canned vegetables are favored over local produce, and citrus fruit is flown in from California and Florida while local fruit rots on the trees. Other imports include such staples as frozen meat, butter, eggs, and pinto beans. To its credit, the government is trying to reverse this trend by offering tax and other incentives to spur production. Locally grown rice is now being marketed by the government under the name *Arroz D'Aqui* ("rice from here"). In spite of these measures, it will be decades before the island can feed itself.

Vieques

THE PEOPLE

Caribbean culture is truly creole culture. The world "creole" comes from *criar* (Spanish for "to bring up" or "rear"). In the New World, this term came to refer to children born in this hemisphere, implying that they were not quite authentic or pure. Later, creole came to connote "mixed blood," but not just blood has been mixed here—cultures have been jumbled as well. Because of this extreme mixture, the Caribbean is a cultural goldmine. The culture of a specific island or nation depends upon its racial mix and historical circumstances. Brought over on slave ships—where differences of status were lost and cultural institutions shattered—the slaves had to begin anew. In a similar fashion but not nearly to so severe a degree, the European, indentured or otherwise, could not bring all of Europe with him. Beliefs were merged in a new synthesis born of the interaction between different cultures— African and European. Today, a new synthesis has arisen in language, society, crafts, and religion: one which has been shaped by and which reflects historical circumstance.

native Indian influence: Although the Indians have long since vanished, their spirit lives on—in tradition, in the feeling of dramatic sunsets, and in the wafting of the cool breeze. Remaining cultural legacies include foods (*achiote*), place names (Mayaguez, Utuado, and Humacao—to name a few), and words (such as "hammock"—an Indian invention), and in native medicines still in use. Even the Indian name for the island, Boriquen, is still popular. Many Spanish towns were built on old Indian sites; the *bateyes* of the Indians became the plazas of the Spanish. There are numerous archaeological sites, most notably those at Utuado and Tibes.

African influence: This was the strongest of all outside influences on those islands with large black populations. Arriving slaves had been torn away from both tribe and culture, and this is reflected in everything from the primitive agricultural system to the African influence on religious sects and cults, mirroring the dynamic diversity of W. African culture. Puerto Rico was a special case in that there were never a large num-

ber of slaves imported and all escaped slaves from other islands who landed on its shores were granted freedom.

Spanish influence: Spain was the original intruder in the
area. Although the Spaniards exited Puerto Rico in 1898, after
400 years of influence, the island's culture is still predominantly Spanish—as are neighboring Cuba and the Dominican
Republic. Most Caribbean islands, whether the Spaniards ever
settled there or not, still bear the names Columbus bestowed
on them 500 years ago. And, although other European influences have had a powerful effect, Spanish continues to be the
predominant language in the islands once controlled by Spain.
Major Spanish architectural sites remain in the old parts of
San Juan and in Santo Domingo, Dominican Republic.

American influence: The history of the U.S. is inextricably
linked with the Caribbean in general and Puerto Rico in particular. American influence in Puerto Rico predates American
occupation. Television and fast food continue to have their effect as have the migration and return of Puerto Ricans to the
mainland.

The Puerto Ricans

Like so many of the neighboring islands, Puerto Rico has
forged a unique racial and cultural mix. The original inhabitants of the island, the Taino Indians, were forced into slavery.
Some escaped into the mountains, where they intermarried
with the local Spanish immigrant subsistence farmers. The
offspring from those unions, the *jibaro*, the barefoot-but-proud
peasant, have come to be regarded as a symbol of the island.
The name itself comes from the *Jivaro*, a fiercely independent
tribe of Amazonian Indians; they lived a highly individualistic
and rugged existence. Residing in *bohios* (thatch huts), they
were virtually self sufficient and skilled in the production of
crafts. With the urbanization and industrialization which
have marked the 20th century, the *jibaros* have dwindled in
numbers to emerge as a prototypical folk hero much like the
American cowboy. Black slaves, although never arriving in the

Street musicians, San Juan

numbers that they did on surrounding islands, added another
important ingredient to the racial-cultural stew. But Puerto
Rico's complex cultural blend doesn't stop there. French families arrived from Haiti and Louisiana in the late 18th and
19th centuries. Loyalist Spaniards and Venezuelans sought
refuge here from newly independent Latin American repub-
lics. A flourishing sugar economy attracted Scottish and Irish
farmers. After abolition, farmers and laborers emigrated from
Spain's NW province of Galicia and the Canary Islands. Chinese coolies were imported in the 1840s to help build roads,
and numbers of Italians, Corsicans, Germans, and Lebanese
also arrived. American expatriates founded an Episcopal
church in Ponce in 1873, and many more arrived after the

American annexation in 1898. Cubans fleeing Castro arrived in the 1960s, as did Dominicans following the 1965 upheavals. Both of these have had a powerful influence: the Cubans at the top social stratum, the Dominicans on the very bottom. All of the diverse ethnic groups, intermarrying and multiplying, have helped forge modern Puerto Rican culture.

population: With 3.4 million people, Puerto Rico is one of the most crowded islands in the world. Its population density of over 1,000 persons per sq mile is higher than any of the 50 States. And still another two million Puerto Ricans live within the continental United States. In fact, more Puerto Ricans reside in New York City than in San Juan. Most have been compelled to migrate by economic necessity; in recent years, however, declining economic opportunities in the States have reversed the trend, and many Puerto Ricans are returning to the island.

social values: Of course, no single description fits all Puerto Ricans; there are too many kinds of people for one mold to apply. And the impact of American colonialism, coupled as it has been with transmigration from the States, has had an immense effect. Social values are undergoing a rapid transformation as the economic base changes from agriculture to industry and manufacturing. Speaking in terms of the traditional culture, however, Puerto Ricans live in a tightly knit, class-structured society. Very conscious of their roles within that society, they submit passively to it. This attitude, which some have termed fatalistic, has deep historic roots. The centuries-old feudal system of social relationships under which the island has been governed continues to this day. Hacienda owners traditionally held immense power over the *agregados*, the landless peons on his property, and the Puerto Rican version of Catholicism has also worked to keep the peasants' aspirations in check: the world was seen as being ruled by supernatural forces, basically benevolent but beyond man's control. *"Acepto lo que Dios me mande,"* ("I accept whatever God will offer me") has been a common expression for generations, as is *"Ay Bendido!"*, an utterance which is short for "Blessed is the Lord," but whose actual meaning is closer to "Ah, woe is me." This sense of resignation seems to pervade social interactions: Puerto Ricans are reluctant to say no, and direct confrontations are avoided. One tries to do things *a la buena*, "the nice way." Resistance is undertaken via the *pelea monga*, literally "the relaxed fight," or passive non-cooperation. Puerto Ricans are very gregarious, but they are also highly independent. Their sensitivity to criticism, and their awareness that individual aims may best be achieved through collective efforts, helps keep them in line. One's expectations in life and one's behavior are formed and controlled by the ever-watchful eyes of one's peers. Social mobility is limited; behavior expected of persons at each class level is clearly defined and taught from birth. All of these factors.combine to help the society run smoothly. Puerto Ricans in general accept their situation; the sense of being small and anonymous and not in direct control of their lives alleviates frustration and works to reinforce traditional customs and conventions.

compadrazgo: Literally "co-parentage," this important practice of social bonding resembles the system of godparents found in the States, but is much more solemn. Selected when a child is baptized, *compadres* and *comadres* can be counted on to help out financially in a pinch. A poor farmer may seek out a rich employer to be his child's compadre. The employer will assent because he knows that this will tighten the bonds between himself and his employee. Or such a relationship may be sought merely to cement a close friendship between males.

males in the society: Although Puerto Rico is indisputably a male-dominated society (as are all Latin cultures), men raised in the traditional culture have tended to be very immature. Women have been instructed to search for a mate who is *serio* (serious), but such men are rare because they are raised to be insecure and unstable. Much effort is made to form "de confianza" (confidential) relationships with other men, and exhibitionism is one way to do this. Fighting, heavy drinking, betting, and sexual prowess are all viewed positively by traditional male society. Sexual experience, both premarital and extramarital, is mandatory for establishing and maintaining one's *macho* status. In Puerto Rico's highly structured pecking order, women are at the bottom.

females in the society: Women are carefully groomed for their role from an early age. Soon after birth their ears are pierced and they begin wearing clothes, whereas their brothers may run around naked for some years. They are carefully separated from contact with the opposite sex; this guarding intensifies as the girls reach puberty. Traditionally, women were considered eligible for marriage at 15 or 16. All chances for girls and boys to meet were carefully controlled. Before *noviazgo* (engagement) there was little chance for them to talk to each other. *Noviazgo* differed from its English equivalent in that it implied a very serious commitment to marry and, accordingly, was very difficult to break. During the period of *noviazgo* the couple were never left alone; the assumption was that they were not to be trusted. Rather than spending the time trying to get to know each other better, the woman was expected only to learn how to accommodate herself to the will of her future husband. Even today, Puerto Rican society fosters a cult of virginity: the woman must be a virgin at marriage. The husband's authority is paramount in the home; the wife controls little money and has no right to make decisions. Husbands dictate; wives submit. Obedience rather than communication is of paramount importance. Because the man has taken her virginity, he owes her support and fair treatment. On the other hand, the wife is forbidden to associate with any other man, even on a casual basis. Women are simply not trusted around men. However, these days attitudes are changing rapidly. Among younger couples there is much better communication between husband and wife, and her status has improved tremendously. The problems of sexual discrimination, however, still remain.

attitudes towards Americans: Puerto Ricans may be numbered among the most hospitable people on Earth. A foreigner will not be long in a bar before someone is buying him a drink and conversing with him. However, a *gringo* may rest assured that he will always be regarded as a *gringo*. Although Puerto Ricans are American citizens and one-third of all Puerto Ricans live in the U.S., the visiting North American will be called *Americano*. Puerto Ricans are clearly doubtful and confused about their political identity, as soon becomes evident in conversation. Puerto Ricans returning from the States are termed *Neoricans* and never completely readmitted into the society.

racial attitudes: As in all of the Caribbean islands, racial prejudice is part of a lingering colonial legacy. Although most Puerto Ricans have at least a pinch of *negrito* blood running through their veins, it is not socially desirable to admit it; the undesirability of being black stems from the fact that the blacks were once slaves. While the apartheid system of the American South never took root here, and Puerto Ricans do not believe in a biological inferiority of blacks, blacks are nevertheless stereotyped as being lower class and it is difficult for them to rise within the society. Traditionally, upper and middle-class islanders have been the most concerned about *limpieza de sangre* (purity of blood), and in the past, trials to prove purity of blood were conducted before an upper-class couple could marry. Today, although prejudice remains, it has been moderated over time: an upper-class man, for example, may marry a mulatto woman without much censure, but she may never be fully accepted by the wives of his associates. Factors such as economic position and social standing now tend to override racial considerations. Still, the darker child in a family may win less praise from his parents and be more likely to be teased by his brothers and sisters. Interestingly enough, the term *negrito,* as used in society, is a term of endearment, implying a sense of community or communal belonging, while *blanquito* ("little white") usually implies the opposite. The latter term has historical roots: *Peninsulares,* islanders born in Spain, held a higher rank than *criollos,* Spaniards born on the island. Today, this term is still used in reference to the elite. The vast majority of Puerto Ricans today are neither black nor white, but *trigueno*—tan or swarthy in color.

Language

Spanish is the norm throughout the island. Although many Puerto Ricans can speak English, the more Spanish the visitor

SPANISH FOR DRIVERS

Adelante	Ahead
Calle sin Salida	Dead end
Peligro	Danger
Desvio	Detour
Salida	Exit
Neblina	Fog
Lomo	Hill or Bump
Desprendimiento	Landslide
A la izquierda	To the left
Puente Estrecho	Narrow bridge
Transito	One way traffic
No Estacione	No parking
Cruce de Peatones	Pedestrian crossing
A la derecha	To the right
Carretera Cerada	Road closed
Zona Escolar	School zone
Semaforo	Signal light
Resbala Mojado	Slippery when wet
Baden	Speed bump
Pare	Stop
Peaje	Toll station
No Vire	No turn
Ceda	Yield

can speak the better—outsiders who can speak Spanish are more readily accepted by locals. The Spanish here is laden with borrowed English (*el coat*, for example), local idioms, and numerous Indian and African words. When speaking with Puerto Ricans, keep in mind that the *"tu"* form of address connotes a high degree of familiarity; don't jump from the more formal *"usted"* until the relationship warrants it. "S" sounds are muted and may even disappear (as in *graciah* instead of *gracias*). The "ll" and "y" sounds are pronounced like the English "j." And the terminal "e" sound is often truncated (as in *noch* instead of *noche*).

RELIGION

Catholicism: Although Puerto Rico is predominantly Catholic, its brand is a far cry from the dogmatic religion practiced in Italy. Distance, combined with the elitist attitudes of the all-Spanish clergy who chose to support slavery and exclude locals from the priesthood, have altered the religion here.

Puerto Ricans have selected the rules and regulations they wish to follow while conveniently ignoring the rest. To them, being a good Catholic does not mean being dogmatic. Many strict Catholic couples, for example, have civil or consensual marriages and practice birth control.

Protestantism: Many other sects have proliferated here as well. Chief among these is Protestantism. Although the religion had reached the island prior to 1898, the U.S. invasion spurred a rapid increase in its popularity. Facilitated by the separation of church and state decreed in the U.S. Constitution, its emphasis on the importance of the individual, so much more in keeping with present-day society than the Catholic emphasis upon dogmatic ritual, won it many new converts. Also, because it provides the rural and urban poor a sense of emotional security in the face of a rapidly changing world, evangelical fundamentalism has also gained in popularity. Presently 1,500 evangelical churches dot the island and missionaries are sent to Europe and Africa to propagate the faith.

Spiritualism

As in other Latin areas, Catholicism has been lightly seasoned with a mixture of African and native Indian traditions. For example, the African influence on the costumes and statues in Loiza Aldea's patron saint festival is unmistakable, as is the dark-colored skin of the Virgin of Monserrate. Some go so far as to claim that spiritualism (*espiritismo*) is the real religion of Puerto Rico. Illegal under Spanish rule, spiritualism surfaced only in this century. Many middle-class Catholics, while remaining formally within the confines of Catholicism, practice spiritualism at home. Few Protestants, on the other hand, are spiritualists because the stress on application of ethical choices in day-to-day existence inherent in Protestantism runs counter to the spiritualist belief that one's fate is affected by

Church of San Jose, San Juan

outside influences or by acts committed in a past existence. Spiritualism is steeped in native Indian religion and folklore. The Tainos believed that *jipia* (spirits of the dead), slept by day and roamed the island by night, eating wild fruit and visiting relatives. Food was always left on the table because easily insulted *jipia* might haunt one's dreams at night if left unfed. Although many no longer know where the belief comes from, plastic fruit is still left atop refrigerators to appease hungry *jipia.* Folk beliefs continue to predominate among country folk. Many still believe in the *mal de ojo* or "evil eye." Although its possessor may be unaware of its power, one covetous glance upon a child, adult, or animal, is believed to cause sickness or even death. Children have been traditionally protected by a bead-charm bracelet. Spiritualism is also closely connected with folk medicine and healing. One should not mix "cold" things with "hot," or touch "cold" things when one is "hot," or he risks suffering *empache* or *espasmo*—stomach cramps or muscular disturbances. "Cold" food, banana or pork for example, must never be mixed with hot food like meat or manioc. One should never wash clothes in a "cold" area while one is "hot," and one should avoid taking a cold bath after getting heated up through physical exercise. *Botanica,* the supermarkets of spiritualism, sell plants, herbs, oils, rubbing water, and spiritualist literature.

santos cults: Another complement to Catholicism is the half-magical cult of the saints or santos. Most households have an image of one or two of these (see "Arts and Crafts"), usually St. Anthony and one of the Virgins. These are grouped together with the family crucifix and designated as the "Holy Family." Saints are selected in accordance with one's needs, and reciprocation is mandatory if devotions are to continue. The relation between saint and worshipper is one of *promesa* (promise or obligation); promises are made by the devotee and carried out if wishes are granted by the saint. Certain goods are offered to the saint, who is expected to reciprocate by providing prosperity and good fortune. Gamblers and drinkers offer up dice, cards, pennies, small glasses of rum, lottery numbers, and pictures of beautiful women to their patron San Expedito. If the saint does not respond, the icon may be beaten and kicked out of the house. Rituals of devotion, termed rosarios, are held to obtain relief from sickness or give thanks for recovery after an illness. Traditional events involving mass participation, such as the Rosario de la Cruz (see "events" under "Bayamon") and the *rogativa* or candlelight procession, are on the wane, as are *valadas,* or pre-funeral wakes in which neighbors gather at the home of a dying community member to render assistance in case of need.

ARTS AND CRAFTS

Puerto Rico's art reflects its cultural diversity. With a growing coterie of young, dynamic artists, the island also has an indigenous crafts tradition rooted in European, African, and Taino tradition. The best places to see art (and antiques) are in the numerous art galleries located in San Juan. A good assortment of crafts can be found at the Folk Arts Center inside the Dominican Convent at Plaza San Jose in Old San Juan. Other shops are located inside Sixto Escobar Stadium near the Caribe Hilton and inside Plazoleta de la Puerto across from Terminal Turismo in Old San Juan. Crafts are sold every weekend along Callejon de la Capilla in Old San Juan as well as El Centro market inside Condado Convention Center. Annual crafts fairs are held on the grounds of the Bacardi Rum Plant, Catano, San Juan, and in Barranquitas. By far the best way to see local crafts, however, is by checking out the island craftspeople in their workshops. Hammock-making is centered in and around San Sebastian. Hats are made in Agua and Moca. Other Puerto Rican crafts include ceramics, masks, musical instruments, wooden replicas of birds and flowers, and macrame. Two of the most important craft traditions, *santos* and *mundillo,* are described below.

santos: Among the oldest and certainly the most impressive of Puerto Rican traditional crafts are santos, eight- to 20-in.-tall figurines representing saints, carved of capa or cedar wood, stone, clay, or gold. While the oldest date back to the 16th C., the *santerio's* craft is a continuation of the indigenous

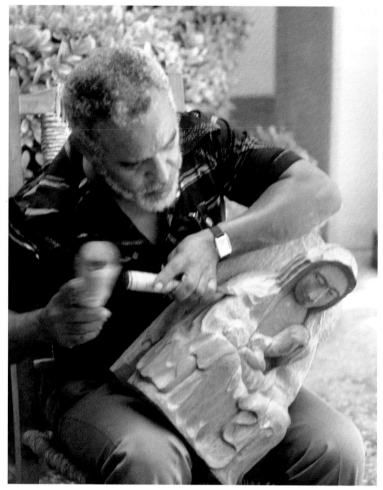

Santos carver, Old San Juan

Indian tradition in which small statues (*zemi*) were placed in every home and village as objects of veneration. Thus, the carving of *santos* seems to be linked to the pre-Columbian era. Just as every town had its patron saint, so every home had its *santos* who would offer protection. And just as some people substitute a TV service for a visit to church, so Puerto Ricans substitute *santos* worship for the traditional Mass. *Santeros,* skilled carpenters using handmade tools, carved the statues out of wood, using natural dyes and sometimes even human hair to decorate them. Natural dyes were subsequently replaced by oils; the initial full-figure design was later joined by carvings of busts and group figures. Saints most commonly represented include the various Virgins (Pilar, Monserrate, Carmen, etc.) and the male saints (Jose, Rafael, Peter the Apostle, etc.). Accompanying symbols render them easily identifiable—just as Rafael carries his spear and fish trademark, so the Virgin of Monserrate holds the baby Jesus on her lap and Saint Anthony is always shown with the infant Jesus and a book. Most popularly represented of the group figures are the Three Kings; others include the Nativity, the Trinity, and biblical scenes. Most remarkable of all the santos is the carving of the *mano pederosa* ("powerful hand"), a hand with five fingers terminating in intricately carved miniature images of various saints. Although *santos*-making reached its artistic peak around the turn of the 20th century, *santeros* still practice their art at various locations all over the island. The best collections of antique *santos* may be seen in Old San Juan. The *santos* possess a singularly attractive and simple solemnity which remains as freshly inspiring today as the day they were carved. Unfortunately, it's difficult to find *santos* of similar quality being carved today and, new or antique, they are expensive.

mundillo: A Spanish import, this type of lacemaking derives its name from the *mundillo* frame on which it is worked. Today, this technique of bobbin lacemaking, which has a 500-year tradition, can be found only in Spain and in Puerto Rico. *Torchon,* or beggar's lace, was the technique first introduced and the one which still predominates today. Originally poorly made and of low quality, it has evolved into a highly intricate and delicate art form. The two traditional styles of lace bands are *entredos,* which have two straight borders, and *puntilla* with a straight and scalloped border. Although the craft once seemed destined to disappear from the island, today it is undergoing a revival. Probably the foremost instructor in San Juan is Maria A. Capella Ricci. One place to see *mundillo* is at the Puerto Rico Weaving Festival held annually at the end of April in Isabela. Otherwise, check the Folk Arts Center at the Dominican Convent (tel. 724-6250) for information on shops which make and sell *mundillo*.

art and artists: Expanding quickly after a belated start, Puerto Rican art has grown to include a wide range of artistic media including mural art, innovative ceramics, and poster art. The story of Puerto Rican art begins with painter Jose Campeche (1751-1809); indeed, painting on the island can hardly be said to have existed before him. His works, which deal exclusively with religious themes, are easily identified through their characteristic style. A self-trained artist who mixed his own pigments, Campeche is today recognized as one of the great artists of the Americas. The next painter to hit the big time was Francesco Oller (1833-1917). Studying art in France and Spain, he returned to the island to create many masterpieces. Known as the first Latin American impressionist, this contemporary of Pissarro and Cezanne was commissioned by King Alfonso of Spain to be Court Painter for six years. An artistic renaissance took place during the 1950s when many artists returned to the island after studying in the States. During this period, poster art emerged as an important medium of artistic expression. Another art form which has gained popularity in recent years is the mural. Mural art, which draws on everything from complex Taino symbology to religious themes, decorates the sides of buildings of all sizes and shapes. Modern Puerto Rican artists of note include Carlos Irizarry, Carlos Osorio, Julio Rosado del Valle, Rafael Turfino, Lorenzo Homar, Carlos Raquel Riviera, and Julio Rosado del Valle.

MUSIC AND DANCE

Although many legacies of European, African, and Taino traditions survive in Puerto Rico, none are as expressive of cultural feeling or as illustrative of intercultural blending as music and dance. The story of Puerto Rican music begins with the Taino. At least one instrument, the *guiro* or *guicharo,* a hollow, notched, bottle-shaped gourd played with a wire fork, has been handed down by the Indians, and musicologists speculate that the *areytos* (Indian dance tunes) have also influenced the development of Puerto Rican music. Besides the Indians, Spanish influence is also evident in the design of musical instruments. Puerto Ricans have transformed the six-string Spanish guitar into four different instruments: the *tiple, cuatro, bordonua,* and *requinto,* which differ in shape, pitch, and number of strings. The ten-string *cuatro,* so named because it is tuned in fourths, is the most popular instrument today. Other instruments include the *maracas,* round gourds filled with small beans or pebbles, and the *tambor,* a hollowed tree trunk with an animal skin stretched on top. Bands of troubadours once traveled from town to town like European wandering minstrels.

folk music: This is varied and multifarious. The *seis* is probably the liveliest and most popular of all Puerto Rican music. Originally limited to six couples, its more than 40 versions, composed of eight-syllable lines, range from contemporary to century-old standards. While some are representative of particular areas (*seis Bayamones* from Bayamon, for example), others are representative of the way the music is danced to. Their names may derive from the area or region from where the dance originated, the style of dance, or after their composers or most famous performers. A story set to song, the *decima* may carry a deep message. *Decimas* are strictly metered into 10-line stanzas controlled by eight-syllable lines and alternating rhyme structure. Another of the more popular forms of Puerto Rican music is the *danza.* Created in the 1850s, its refined, classical score resembles a minuet; the *danza* is a uniquely Puerto Rican musical interpretation of this Spanish Caribbean form. Juan-Morel Campos, known as the father of the *danza,* is the best-known early composer. The most famous composer of popular music is Rafael Hernandez who died in 1966. Known for such hits as "El Cumbanchero" and "Lamento Borincano," Hernandez is idolized on the island.

bomba y plena: These two most famous types of music coupled with dance are usually grouped together although in real-

Dancing *plena*

ity they are totally different forms. While the *plena* possesses
the elegance and coquetry of the Spanish tradition the *bomba*
has the beat of Africa. Though the origin of both the *bomba*
and the *plena* is uncertain, some maintain that their arrange-
ments were influenced by the Taino *areytos* (epic songs danced
to by the Indians); certainly both are a mixture of European
and African influences—although African elements predominate in the *bomba*. Some say that the *plena* was brought to the
island by a couple from St. Kitts. Historians do agree, however,
that the *plena* first emerged in Ponce. Once an important social event, the *bomba* provided the working people the only
available relief from the monotonous drudgery of everyday life.
Usually on Saturday or Sunday nights or on special occasions

and festivities, the dance was performed in a circle. The soloist stood next to the drums, and the chorus stood behind the singer. While the soloist sang, the chorus provided the harmonies. The dancer, entering in front of the drums, performed the *piquete* (coquettish dance) before saluting the drums and exiting. The *bomba* is really a dialogue between drummer and dancer. The first drummer (*repicador*) challenges the dancer to a duel while the second drummer maintains the basic rhythmic pattern. The dance lasts as long as the dancer can successfully challenge the drummer. Unlike similar dances found elsewhere, the drummer follows the dancer rather than vice-versa. The different rhythms of the *bomba* (the *Cunya, Yuba, Cuende, Sica, Cocobale, Danua, Holande,* etc.) represent the diverse ethnic roots of the dance. While the first five are African names, the latter two represent adaptations of Danish and Dutch styles learned from arriving immigrants. Another style, *Lero,* is an adaption of the French circle dance, *le rose.*

symphonic music: Interest in classical music has grown over the years in Puerto Rico, and the island has its own symphony orchestra and conservatory. A great inspiration was cellist and conductor Pablo Casals who retired at age 81 to the island, his mother's birthplace, to spend his last years there. Each year the month-long Casals Festival draws artists from all over the world to perform his music. The most notable native classical musician was master pianist Jesus Maria Sanroma (1902–1984) who toured and recorded internationally. A friend and collaborator of Casal's, he promoted both symphonic music on the island and the *danza*—recording, editing, and performing the latter. Puerto Rico is also the birthplace of famed operatic tenor Antonio Paoli (1872–1946) who performed for Czar Nicholas II of Russia, Kaiser Wilhelm of Germany, and the Emperor Franz Joseph of Austria. The latter bestowed upon him the title of Court Singer. After earning and spending an estimated $2 million, Paoli returned home to the island in 1922 where he taught music to the island's youth. Other famous Puerto Rican opera singers include Pablo Elvira and Justino Diaz.

modern music: Although born and bred in New York's Caribbean melting pot, salsa (Spanish for "sauce") and the

Dominican-originated merengue blare from every car stereo and boom box on the island. El Gran Combo, led by pianist Rafael Ithier, is one of Puerto Rico's contributions to the salsa scene. Major salsa figures of Puerto Rican extraction include pianists (and brothers) Charlie and Eddie Palmieri, trombonist Willie Colon, percussionist Ray Barretto, and timbale wizard Tito Puente. Born in Ponce, Jose "Cheo" Feliciano is one of the most famous island-born salsa singers.

FESTIVALS AND EVENTS

The Latin nature of the island really comes to the fore in its celebration of festivals and holidays. Puerto Ricans really know how to relax and have a good time. Although the centuries-old custom of midday siesta is in danger of extinction, *Viernes social* or "social Friday" is still popular. Every Friday men gather and eat *lechon asado* (roast pig) and gossip and gamble at local roadside stands. Most other celebrations, however, are in a religious vein. Many of these are famous, including those at Hormigueros and Loiza; the 24 of June Festival of St. John the Baptist in San Juan is one long night of partying. Every town on the island has its *fiesta patronales* or patron saint festival. They always begin on a Friday, approximately 10 days before the date prescribed. Although services are held twice a day, the atmosphere is anything but religious. Music, gambling, and dancing take place on the town plaza, and food stalls sell local specialties. On the Sunday nearest the main date, *imahenes* or wooden images of the patron saint are carried around the town by four men or (sometimes) women. Flowers conceal supporting wires, and the base is tied to the platform to prevent it from falling. A generally somber atmosphere prevails during Holy Week (*Semana Santa*), the week surrounding Easter, when processions and pageants are held island-wide. Las Navidades or the Christmas season, which stretches from 15 Dec. to 6 Jan., is the liveliest time of the year. Marked by parties and prayers, it's a time to get together with friends. Everyone heads for *el campo* ("the country") to join in celebrating the occasion with friends and loved ones. Out in the countryside, groups of local musicians known as *trulla* roam from house to house singing *aguinaldos* or Christmas carols. *Nacimento* (nativity scenes) are set up in homes and public places, the most famous being the one near San Cristobal fortress in Old San Juan. On *Nocho Bueno* (Christmas Eve) most people attend midnight Mass (*Misa de Gallo*) before returning home to feast on the traditional large supper known as cena. On 6 Jan. *Epiphany* or Three Kings Day is celebrated. The night before, children traditionally place boxes of grass under their beds to await the arrival of the Three Kings, Gaspar, Melchior, and Baltazar. After the camels eat all the grass, the kings leave presents in the now empty boxes. On the day itself, the Three Kings are put up in front of the Capitol building, and candy and toys are given away on the grounds of El Morro fortress in Old San Juan.

Puerto Rico Festivals and Events

1 Jan.: New Year's Day

6 Jan.: Epiphany or Three Kings Day; traditional day of gift-giving

11 Jan.: Birthday of Eugenio De Hostos, Puerto Rican educator, writer, and patriot (half-day)

15 Jan.: Martin Luther King Birthday (half-day)

18–20 Jan.: San Sebastian Street Fiesta in Old San Juan. Crafts, shows, arts, games, processions, dancing, and *paso fino* horses on display.

Feb.: Washington's Birthday (half-day, movable)

22 March: Emancipation Day

April: Good Friday (movable)

16 April: Jose de Diego's Birthday

May: Memorial Day (movable)

24 June: St. John the Baptist Day

4 July: Independence Day

17 July: Luiz Munoz Rivera's Birthday

25 July: Commonwealth Constitution Day

27 July: Dr. Jose Celso Barbosa's Birthday (half-day)

Sept.: Labor Day (movable)

Oct.: Columbus Day (movable)

11 Nov.: Veterans' Day

19 Nov.: Puerto Rico Discovery Day

Nov.: Thanksgiving (movable)

25 Dec.: Christmas Day

PRACTICALITIES

Transport

by air: Although the days of bargain basement flights are over, it's still possible to visit Puerto Rico relatively cheaply. And though the only really cheap way to get there is to swim, you can still save money by shopping around. A good travel agent should call around for you to find the lowest fare; if he or she doesn't, find another agent, or try doing it yourself. If there are no representative offices in your area, check the phone book—most airlines have toll-free numbers. In these days of airline deregulation, fares change quicker than you can say *"Menudo,"* so it's best to check the prices well before departure—and then again before you go to buy the ticket. Seven-day APEX (advance purchase excursion) fares, weekday and night flights, and one-way fares are among the options that may save you money. The more flexible you can be about when you wish to depart and return, the easier it will be to find a bargain. Whether dealing with a travel agent or with the airlines themselves make sure that you let them know clearly what it is you want. Don't assume that because you live in Los Angeles, for example, it's cheapest to fly from

TRAVEL DISTANCES IN PUERTO RICO

(top number—km; bottom number—miles)

	Aguadilla	Arecibo	Caguas	Cayey	Coamo	Fajardo	Guayama	Humacao	Manati	Mayaguez	Ponce	San German	San Juan	San Sebastian	Yauco
Aguadilla		53	149	161	138	180	162	177	79	28	104	47	136	25	74
		33	93	101	86	112	101	110	49	17	65	29	85	16	46
Arecibo	53		96	108	91	127	133	124	26	72	82	93	83	41	82
	33		60	67	57	79	83	77	16	45	51	58	52	25	51
Caguas	149	96		26	61	54	53	28	70	172	95	152	35	137	126
	93	60		16	38	34	33	17	43	107	59	94	22	85	78
Cayey	161	108	26		35	80	27	54	82	146	69	126	52	148	100
	100	67	16		22	50	17	34	51	91	43	78	32	92	62
Coamo	138	91	61	35		115	42	89	65	111	34	91	80	113	65
	86	57	38	22		71	26	55	40	69	21	57	50	70	40
Fajardo	180	127	54	80	115		92	33	101	199	149	206	59	168	180
	112	79	34	50	71		57	21	63	124	93	128	37	104	112
Guayama	162	133	53	27	42	92		59	107	135	58	116	79	137	89
	101	83	33	17	26	57		37	66	84	36	72	49	85	55
Humacao	177	124	28	54	89	33	59		98	194	117	174	60	165	148
	110	77	17	34	55	21	37		61	121	73	108	37	103	92
Manati	79	26	70	82	65	101	107	98		98	82	119	57	67	108
	49	16	43	51	40	63	66	61		61	51	74	35	42	67
Mayaguez	28	72	172	146	111	199	135	194	98		77	19	155	31	46
	17	45	107	91	69	124	84	121	61		48	12	96	19	29
Ponce	104	82	95	69	34	149	58	117	82	77		57	114	79	31
	65	51	59	43	21	93	36	73	51	48		35	71	49	19
San German	47	93	152	126	91	206	116	174	119	19	57		171	52	26
	29	58	94	78	57	128	72	108	74	12	35		106	32	16
San Juan	136	83	35	52	80	59	79	60	57	155	114	171		124	145
	85	52	22	32	50	37	49	37	35	96	71	106		77	90
San Sebastian	25	41	137	148	113	168	137	165	67	31	79	52	124		64
	16	25	85	92	70	104	85	103	42	19	49	32	77		40
Yauco	74	82	126	100	65	180	89	148	108	46	31	26	145	64	
	46	51	78	62	40	112	55	92	67	29	19	16	90	40	

there. It may be better to find an ultrasaver flight to gateway cities like New York or Miami and then change planes. Fares tend to be cheaper on weekdays and during low season (mid-April to mid-December). The lowest fare you can hope to get out of New York City is in the range of $129 OW, $210 RT; from Miami, about $129 OW, $258 RT; and from Atlanta, $173 OW, $281 RT. Delta flies directly from Atlanta (3½ hours), Eastern Airlines flies direct from New York, Newark, Atlanta, and Miami. They offer a bewildering variety of APEX fares, so check to find the most convenient. Puerto Rico may also be reached by air from everywhere in the Caribbean except Cuba.

by sea: Sadly, there's no passenger service between Puerto Rico and other Caribbean islands. In 1987 a hydrofoil ran to the Virgin Islands, but as it was designed more for use in rivers than at sea, it soon folded. And there may be a catamaran service available to St. Thomas. So, unless you are willing to take a cruise ship—which not only costs more than flying but often isolates you from locals—there is no regularly scheduled alternative. One potentially rewarding opportunity if you can afford it is to sail your own yacht to Caribbean waters and travel about on your own. Or fly to St. Thomas or Tortola and

AIRLINES (*LINEAS AEREAS*)	
AIRLINE	**TELEPHONE NUMBER**
Aero Virgin Islands	791–1215, 791–1216
Air BVI	791–2117
Air France	724–0500
ALM	791–2150, 756–5985
American	721–1747
American Eagle	721–1747
BWIA	724–2555, 791–3613
Delta	721–1011
Dominicana	724–7100
Eastern	728–3131
Eastern Metro	791–4744
Flamenco	724–7110, 725–7707
Iberia	721–5630, 791–0078
LACSA	(800) 225–2272, 791–6400
LIAT	791–3838
Lufthansa	723–9553
Mexicana	721–2323
Panamena	725–4815
TWA	(800) 892–8466
VIASA	721–3340
Vieques Air Link	722–3736
Virgin Islands Seaplane Shuttle	(800) 595–9504, 791–1455

rent a yacht to sail to Puerto Rico. It's possible to crew on a boat coming over from Europe; most, however, head for the southern Caribbean, so you'd have to find a way (expensive) north from there.

package tours: As they say, all that glitters is not gold. This cliche may be old but it is certainly pertinent when it comes to package tours. If you want to have everything taken care of, then package tours are the way to go. However, they do have at least two distinct disadvantages: everything (or most things) have already been decided for you which takes much of the thrill out of traveling, and you are more likely to be put up in a large characterless hotel (where the tour operators can get quantity discounts) rather than in a small inn (where you can get quality treatment). So think twice before you sign up. Also, if you should want to sign up, read the fine print and see what's *really* included and what's not! Don't be taken in by useless freebies that gloss over the lack of such things as paid meals.

getting around: You'll need to have patience. Always allow plenty of time to get to any island destination. City bus service in San Juan is cheap but painfully inefficient and slow. Around the island, there is no longer any regular passenger bus service. However, unscheduled but cheap rural services run all over the island, including along the mountain road from Arecibo down to Ponce. *Publicos* are Ford vans with seats which serve as shared taxis. A cheap and convenient form of transportation, they can be picked up or left at any point. Identifiable by the letter "P" on the license plate, their route is listed on the windshield. Unfortunately, except for the San Juan-Ponce and similar San-Juan-originated runs, they cover only short hops between towns, which can mean changing vehicles innumerable times before reaching your final destination. Hitchhiking is slow but very possible and a good way to pass the time while waiting for buses. An alternative to taking local transport or renting a car is the Fondo de Mejoramiento, a local travel organization that conducts tours to various spots of scenic, historical, and cultural interest (tel.

Publico

759–8366). **renting a car:** The island's poor internal transportation system may make renting a car an option you'll want to consider. If you don't have insurance, however, you should definitely make sure you're covered. All too often roads are poorly marked so getting anywhere can be an adventure in itself. Cars may be rented at the airport; a valid U.S. or International driver's license is required. Expect to pay at least $25 per day, but weekend specials may be available. Smaller companies frequently offer better deals. See the chart for listings. As you should do everywhere, read the contract thoroughly— especially the fine print. Ask about unlimited mileage, free gas, late return penalties, and drop-off fees. **internal air transport:** Small airlines fly to the outlying islands of Vieques and Culebra; Eastern and American fly daily from San Juan to Ponce and Mayaguez. **on water:** Passenger ferries leave daily from Fajardo to Culebra and Vieques. Another ferry of note is the Catano Ferry in Old San Juan. Passenger boat service (free) is available on Dos Bocas Lake.

PARADORES AT A GLANCE

These government-sponsored ''country inns'' are scattered all across the island. For current prices and to book reservations, write Paradores Puertorriquenos, Box 4435, Old San Juan, PR 00905. Or call (800) 443–0266. NOTE: *Paradores* located in rural areas require your own transportation. All transportation times given are by private car.

NAME	LOCATION AND FACILITIES
Banos de Coamo	One half hour's drive from Ponce and one and a half hours from San Juan (via the expressway). Facilities include 48 a/c rooms with private bath and balconies, restaurant, hot spring swimming pool, hot springs, tennis court, poolside bar.
Boquemar	In Cabo Rojo, Boqueron, off Carr. 307 and 103. Near Mayaguez, La Parguera, Puerto Real fishing village, and numerous beaches. Facilities include 41 a/c rooms with second floor balcony, refrigerator, and a pool.
Casa Grande	Located on Carr. 612 relatively near Utuado. Facilities include 20 fan-equipped rooms, restaurant, pool, and hiking trails amidst a former coffee plantation.
Guajataca	Two hours from San Juan on Carr. 2, km 103.8 near Quebradillas. Near beach, Lago Guajataca (bring fishing gear), and relatively near Arecibo Observatory and Camuy Caves. Facilities include 38 a/c rooms with private bath and balconies facing the ocean, restaurant, pool, live music on weekends, telephone in room, and two tennis courts.
Hacienda Gripinas	Two and one half hours from San Juan on Carr. 527, km. 2.5 near Jayuya. Near Caguana Ball Park, petroglyphs, and Lago Caonilla (bring fishing gear). Facilities include 19 rooms with private bath and (most) with ceiling fans in 200-year-old restored coffee great house, pool, and restaurant.
Hacienda Juanita	In former coffee plantation two and one half hours from San Juan on Carr. 105, km. 232.5 near Marico town, fish hatchery, and Monte del Estado reserve. Facilities include 21 rooms with private bath, restaurant, lounge, hiking trails and tennis, volleyball, and handball courts.
Martorell	Located 45 minutes from San Juan in Luquilllo near Luquillo Beach, Loiza, and El Yunque. Facilities include seven rooms and hammocks on the premises.
Montemar	Two and one half hours from San Juan at 84 Montemar Ave., Urb. Villa Lydia, Aguadilla. Facilities include 40 a/c rooms with private balconies and bath, two restaurants, live music on weekends, pool, and convention hall.
Oasis	Along Carr. 102 in San German two and one half hours from San Juan near La Parguera, and Mayaguez. Facilities include 34 a/c rooms with private bath and color TV, restaurant, and convention hall.
Posada Porlamar	Two and one half hours from San Juan on Carr. 304 in Lajas near San German and La Parguera. Facilities include 19 a/c rooms, restaurant, and kitchen facilities.
Perichi's	Located at Carr. 102, km 14.3 in San German two and one half hours from San Juan near many beaches, Mayaguez Mall, and San German. Facilities include 15 a/c rooms with private bath and balconies facing the sea, restaurant, basketball court, and dance music on weekends.
El Sol	Located at 9 East Mariano Riera, Plamer Street, Mayaguez. Facilities include 40 a/c rooms with private bath, color cable TV, continental breakfast, and swimming pool.
Villa Antonio	Two and one half hours from San Juan on Carr. 115, km. 12.3 in Rincon, the island's surf capital. Facilities include 50 a/c rooms (cabanas and apartments), two tennis courts, and swimming pool.
Villa Esperanza	Located in Esperanza on Vieques Island near Sunbe beach. Facilities include 50 rooms with private bath and ceiling fans, restaurant, swimming pool, tennis court, and volleyball court.
Villa Parguera	On Carr. 304 in La Parguera, two and one half hours from San Juan. Facilities include 50 a/c rooms with private bath, restaurant, swimming pool, and live floor show and dance music on weekends.
Vistamar	On Carr. 113, km 4 off Carr. 2 two hours from San Juan in Quebradillas near Guajataca Beach and relatively near Arecibo Observatory and Camuy Caves. Facilities include 35 a/c rooms with private bath, restaurant, swimming pool, game room, and tennis, volleyball, and basketball courts.

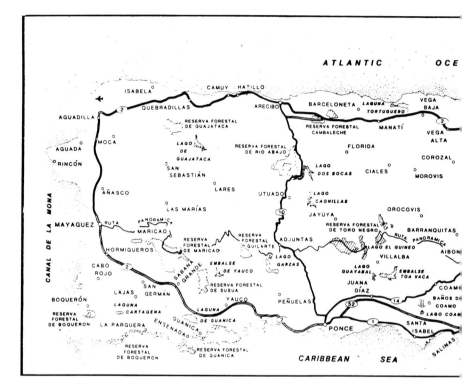

Accommodations

You may wish to breeze by the tourist traps and explore other
areas of the island where things can be much cheaper. **Centros Vacacionales** are clusters of rental cottages situated at
Boqueron, Cabo Rojo, Humacao, Maricao, and Arroyo. These
are available to "bona fide family groups" for $20 per night
with a minimum stay of two and a maximum stay of seven
nights. From 1 Sept. through 31 May there's a special weekly
rate of $100. For more information and a reservation form (apply 120 days in advance) write to Oficina de Reservaciones,
Compania de Fomento Recreativo, Apartado Postal No. 3207,
San Juan, PR 00904 (tel. 722–1771/1551, 721–2800 ext. 225,
275). Attractive buildings set in lush surroundings, the
government-run **paradores** were planned to be inexpensive

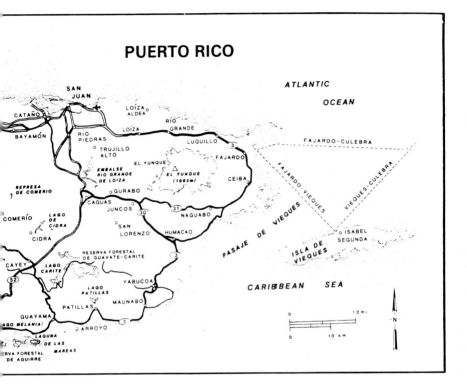

inns originally. Now they're moderately priced and normally empty during the week. Reservations may be made toll free from the States by dialing (800) 443-0266. They may also be made in Old San Juan at 301 San Justo, tel. 721-2400 or 721-2884. The toll free no. within the island is 137-800-462-7575. There are many campgrounds, but take good care that your gear is safe.

apartment and condominium rentals: These are best reserved in advance. Heidi Steiger, 2019 Cacique St., Santurce, PR 00911 (tel. 727-6248), rents high quality apartments in the Condado area. Out in Luquillo, to the E of San Juan, Playa Azul Realty (Box 386, Luquillo, PR 00673, tel. 889-3425) rents out studio, one, two, and three bedroom apartments. Prices range from $300 pw ($800 pm) for a studio to $300 to rent a

three bedroom, two bath for the weekend. Most are air con-
ditioned; all come with fully equipped kitchens; and all
have guard service, face the ocean, and have beach and pool
facilities.

Food and Drink

You'll find plenty of places to eat. There are cafeterias which
serve everything from grilled cheese sandwiches to rice and
beans, simple local restaurants, and their more expensive
cousins which serve the most elaborate combinations of Spanish and other cuisines imaginable. In addition, there are the
ubiquitous fast-food joints and a proliferation of pizzerias.
Combining African, Indian, and Spanish cuisine into something new and refreshingly different, food on the island provides a unique culinary experience. Although similar to
Dominican, Cuban, and other Caribbean cuisines, it has its
own distinct flavor. Seasonings used include pepper, cinnamon,
fresh ginger, cilantro, lime rind, *naranja agria* (sour orange),
and cloves. *Sofrito,* a sauce used to flavor many dishes, com-
bines *achiote* (annato seeds fried in lard and strained) with
ham and other seasonings. Many dishes are cooked in a
caldero, a cast-iron kettle with a rounded bottom.

snacks: Street vendors and *cafeterias* sell a wide variety of
tasty, deep-fried snacks. *Alcapurrias* contain ground plantain
and pork, or (less commonly) fish or crab fried in batter. *Baca-
litos fritos* are fried codfish fritters made with the dried, salted
cod imported from New England. *Amarillos en dulce* are yellow plantains fried in a sauce of cinnamon, sugar, and red
wine. *Empanadas* are made with yuca or plantain dough
stuffed with meat and wrapped in plantain leaves. *Pastelillos*
are fried dough containing meat and cheese. They are sometimes made using fruit and jam; *empanadillas* ("little pies")
are larger versions available on some parts of the island. *Pasteles* are made from plantain or *yautia* dough which has been
stuffed with ground pork, garbanzo beans, and raisins and
wrapped in plantain leaves. *Pinonos* are a mixture of ground

beef and ripe plantains dipped in a beaten egg batter and then fried. *Surullitos* or *sorullos* are deep-fried corn meal fritters. *Rellenos de papa* are meat-stuffed potato balls fried in egg batter. *Mofongo* are mashed and roasted plantain balls made with spices and *chicharron* (crisp pork cracklings).

soups and specialties: Not particularly a vegetable-producing island, Puerto Rico nevertheless has its own unique *verduras* (vegetables), including *chayote* and *calabaza* (varieties of west Indian squash), *yuca* (cassava), *yautia* (tanier), *batata* (a type of sweet potato), and *name* (African yam). All are frequently served in local stews. *Asopao* is a soup made with rice and meat or seafood. *Lechon asado* or roast pig is an island specialty. Served in local *lechonera*, it's tastiest when the pig's skin is truly crisp and golden. *Chicharron,* chunks of crispy skin, are sold alongside. Other pork dishes include *cuchifrito,* pork innards stew, *mondongo* (an African stew of chopped tripe), and *gandinga,* liver, heart, and kidneys cooked with spices. *Carne mechada* is a beef roast garnished with ham, onion, and spices. Goat is also quite popular and cabro (young or kid goat) is considered a delicacy. *Fricase,* a dish made with stewed chicken, rabbit, or goat, is usually accompanied by *tostones,* plantains that have been fried twice. *Sopa de habichuelos negros* (black bean soup), is a popular dish, as are the standards, *arroz con habichuelos* (rice and beans) and *arroz con pollo* (rice and chicken).

seafood: One of the most popular seafood items is actually imported from New England. *Bacalao* (dried, salted codfish) is cooked in several ways. *Bacalao a la Viscaino* is codfish stewed in rich tomato sauce. *Serenata* is flaked bacalao served cold with an oil and vinegar dressing and toppings like raw onions, avocados, and tomatoes. Although some other seafood like shrimp must be imported, many others like *chillo* (red snapper), *mero* (sea bass), *pulpo* (octopus), and *chapin* (trunkfish) are available locally. Fish dishes served *en escabeche* have been pickled Spanish-style. *Ensalada de pulpo* is a tasty salad centering on octopus. *Mojo isleno* is an elaborate sauce which includes olives, onions, tomatoes, capers, vinegar, garlic, and pimentos. The most famous dishes are *langosta* (local lobster), *jueyes* (land crabs), and *ostiones* (miniature oysters which cling to the roots of mangrove trees). The damming of the island's rivers has brought about a decline of another indigenous delicacy, *camarones de rio* (river shrimp).

cheese and sandwiches: *Queso de hoja* is the very milky, mild-flavored local soft cheese. It must be eaten fresh. It is often combined with the local marmalade, *pasta de guayava* (guava paste). Many types of sandwiches are also available. A *cubano* contains ham, chicken, and cheese inside a long, crusty white bread. A *medianoche* ("midnight") contains pork, ham, and cheese.

desserts: Puerto Rican desserts are simple but tasty. They include *arroz con dulce* (sweet rice pudding), *cazuela* (rich pumpkin and coconut pudding), and *bien-me-sabe* (sponge cake with coconut sauce), *tembleque* (coconut pudding), and *flan* (caramel custard).

fruit: Although many fruits are imported from the U.S., Puerto Rico also grows a large variety of its own. Brought by the Spaniards in the 16th C., the sweet orange is known as *china* because the first seeds came from there. Vendors will peel off the skin with a knife to make a *chupon* which you can pop into your mouth piece by piece. *Naranja* is the sour orange. *Guineo* or bananas, imported by the Spanish from Africa, come in all sizes, from the five-inch *ninos* on up. Brought from southern Asia, the *platano* or plantain is inedible until cooked. Puerto Rican *pina* are much sweeter than their exported counterpart because they are left on the stem to ripen. The white interior of the *panapen* or breadfruit is roasted or boiled as a vegetable. Some bear small brown seeds, *panas de pepita*, that are boiled or roasted. Another fruit indigenous to the West Indies, *lechosa* or *papaya* is available much of the year. The oval *parcha* (passion fruit) with its bright orange pulp was given its name by arriving Spaniards who saw its white and purple flowers as a representation of the Crucifixion in botanical form. Coconut palms arrived in 1549 from Cape Verde, Africa, via Dutch Guiana. Other island fruits include the *mamey* (mammee apple), *guanabana* (custard apple), *guava*, *nispero* (sapodilla), *caimito* (star apple), *jobo* (hogplum), and the *jagua* (genipap). The *quenepa* or "Spanish lime" is a

Street vendor, Santurce

Portuguese delicacy about the size of a large walnut; its brittle green skin cracks open to reveal a white pit surrounded by pinkish pulp. Island avocados are renowned for their thick pulp and small seeds. *Acerola*, the wild W. Indian cherry, has from 20–50 times the vitamin C of orange.

drinks: Delicious fruit drinks are made from passion fruit and others. These are usually found at roadside stands in the countryside areas. Lotus is the government brand of delicious canned pineapple juice. Some Puerto Ricans maintain it's the best thing the government does! *Limber* (or *piragua*) is shaved ice covered with tamarind or guava syrup served in a paper cup; it's named after Charles Lindbergh, the famous pilot.

Cool *cocos fríos* or green drinking coconuts are available just about anywhere for around 50¢. *Malta* is a unique-tasting, non-alcoholic malt beverage made with barley, malt, cane sugar, corn grits, and hops. *Maví* is a local root beer made from tree bark.

alcohol: Locally brewed India, Medalla, and Criolla beers are available in seven- and 12-oz. bottles and cans in every colmado or bar. Also available are (German) Tigre beer, Heineken, Schaffer, and Bud. Blue laws are nonexistent in Puerto Rico; alcohol may be purchased anytime, anywhere. Puerto Rico is the world's largest rum producer and accounts for 83% of U.S. sales. Rum production began in the 16th C. with production of *pintriche* or *canita* (bootleg rum), a spirit that is still popular today. Under the Mature Spirits Act, white rum must be distilled for at least one year at a minimum of 180 proof and gold label (amber colored rum) for three years at 175 proof. Anejo, a special blend, requires six years. Although all brands are roughly equivalent, Bacardi is the largest distiller on the island. (See "San Juan Bay and Catano" under "Old San Juan" for tour information). Locals usually drink their rum with ice and water. Drinks such as *pina coladas* and banana daiquiris were developed especially for the tourist trade. *Pina coladas* are made by combining cream of coconut with pineapple juice, rum, and crushed ice. Aside from alcohol, the most popular drink in Puerto Rico must be coffee. It is served either as *cafe* or *cafe con leche* (coffee essence with steamed milk) along with generous quantities of sugar. *Pocillo* or *cafe negro* is a demitasse cup of strong coffee served after dinner.

Sports

swimming: All the island's beaches must have unrestricted access by law. The island's *balnearios* provide lockers, showers, and parking. They are open Tues. to Sun. 9–5 (summer) and 8–5 (winter). A list follows: Playa Escambron, Ave. Munoz Rivera, Puerto de Tierra; Playa Isla Verde, Carr. 187, km. 3.9 (both accessible by city bus); Playa Punta Salinas, Carr. 868, km. 1.2, Catano; Playa Sardinera, Carr. 698, Dorado; Playa Cerro Gordo, Carr. 690, Vega Alta; Playa Luquillo, Carr. 3, km. 35.4; Playa Seven Seas, Carr. 987, Fajardo; Playa Sombe, Carr. 997, Vieques; Playa Punta Santiago, Carr. 3, km. 77, Humacao; Playa Punta Guilarte, Carr. 3, km. 128.5, Arroyo; Playa Cana Gordo, Carr. 333, km. 5.9, Guanica; Playa Boqueron, Carr. 101, Cabo Rojo; Playa Anasco, Carr. 401, km. 1, Anasco.

scuba and snorkeling: Puerto Rico is an exceptionally fine place to do either. A large number of companies offer instruction/rentals. Besides San Juan, scuba is also found in Isabela, Fajardo, and on Culebra and Vieques.

surfing: Most popular location is Rincon. Others include Pine Grove in Isla Verde; Los Aviones in Pinones (E of Isla Verde); Jobos (near Isabela); La Pared (Luquillo); Los Tubos (next to Tortuguero Lagoon in Vega Baja).

wind surfing: Most popular locations include Condado Lagoon, Ocean Park beaches, Boqueron (in the SW) and Ensenada Honda on Culebra.

deep-sea fishing: Thirty world records have been broken with fish caught from the island's seas! You can expect tuna, mackerel, bonefish, yellowfish, blue marlin, wahoo, and tarpon. Half and full-day charters are available. San Juan charters include: San Juan Fishing Charters (tel. 723–0415, 781–7001 evenings); Castillo Watersports (tel. 791–6195, 726–5752 evenings); and Benitez Deep-Sea Fishing (tel. 723–2292, 724–6265). Also try finding a charter at La Parguera in the SW.

lake fishing: Rental equipment is not yet available so bring your own. Try Lago Dos Bocas near Utuado, Lago Cidra, Lago Patillas, Lago Toa Vaca (in Villalba); Lago Yauco; and Lago Guajataca (in Quebradillas). Fish include catfish, peacock bass, largemouth bass, tilapia, and sunfish.

sailing: Boats can be rented at La Playita Boat Rental, 1010 Ave. Ashford, Condado (tel. 722–1607) and the Condado Plaza Hotel Watersports Center (tel. 721–1000, ext. 1361). Rentals are also available at Dorado and Palmas del Mar. **marinas:**

Tourism Fishing Pier, Stop 10, Ave. Fernandez Juncos, Miramar; Isleta Marina (off the coast from Fajardo), tel. 863–0370; Puerto Chico, Carr. 987, Fajardo, tel. 728–2450, 863–5131; Marina de Palmas, Palmas del Mar, Humacao, tel. 852–6000 (ext. 2551). **regattas:** The three-day Velasco Cup Regatta, held in Fajardo in March, marks the start of the Caribbean Ocean Racing Circuit. In July is the Budweiser Around Puerto Rico Race which begins at El Morro in Old San Juan. On Labor Day is the Copa de Palmas held at the Palmas del Mar Resort. In November Fajardo hosts the three-day Kelly Cup Regatta.

tennis: An abundance of courts are found around San Juan. San Juan Central Park, Calle Cerra, has 17 lighted courts (tel.

Palmas del Mar

722–1646). Hotels with courts include Caribe Hilton, Carib Inn, Condado Beach, Condado Plaza, and El San Juan. Out on the island there are courts at the Dorado hotels and at Palmas del Mar Resort; Club Riomar in Rio Grande; Hotel Copamarina (Guanica); and at Punta Borinquen (Aguadilla).

golf: Plenty of places to play including Palmas del Mar Resort and the Dorado hotels. Other courses include the Luis Ortis (in the metropolitan area, tel. 786–3859, 787–7252); Berwind Country Club (in Rio Grande); and at the Mayaguez Hilton.

horseback riding: Available at Palmas del Mar Resort, Santurce's Centro Equestre de Puerto Rico (tel. 728–4530), and at Hacienda Carabali (tel. 795–6351). The Paso Fino Horse Show is held in Guayama in February-March. Post time for racing at El Comandate (tel. 724–6060), to the E of San Juan, is 2:30 on Sun., Wed., Fri., and holidays.

Other Practicalities

money and measurements: Monetary unit is the U.S. dollar (called *"dolar"* or *"peso"*) which is divided into 100 cents (referred to as *"centavos"* or *"chavitos"*). Nickels (5¢) are referred to as *"vellons"* or *"ficha."* Quarters (25¢) are called *"pesetas."* If coming from abroad, it's better to change your money in a major U.S. city or carry traveler's cheques. Deak International, with branches at San Juan International Airport and Terminal Turismo in Old San Juan, issues traveler's cheques commission-free. Measurements are a confusing mixture of American and metric. Gasoline and milk are both sold by the liter (*litro*). While road distances are given in kilometers, road speed signs and car speedometers use miles per hour. Land elevations are expressed in meters, but land is sold in units called cuerda, equal to 97/100 of an acre. Weights are measured in pounds (*libras*) and ounces (*onzas*); a tonelda is a ton. *Pulgadas* are inches, and *pies* are feet.

broadcasting and media: TV serves up a combination of the worst of American programming rendered into Spanish and bad local imitations of the worst of American programming. As is the case with radio and the press, it dishes up AP and UPI stories as news. There are three daily papers: the English tabloid the *San Juan Star,* owned by the Scripps Howard chain, is the least partisan. Superficial and bland, its magazine format provides no investigative reporting. The Knight Chain has engulfed *El Mundo. El Nueva Dia* is the personal property of Luis A. Ferre Enterprises. Almost comically grotesque, *El Vocero,* the newspaper of the masses, is full of really gory, bloody murders, many of which are featured on the cover.

visas: All visitors from abroad (except Canadians) require a U.S. visa. It's better to obtain a multiple entry visa and, if possible, to do so in your own country. Fill out forms perfectly; consular officials tend to be aggravatingly picayune.

health: Medical care is usually on a first-come, first-served basis. Although the quality of medical and dental services is reasonably high, it's not quite up to mainland standards. Most physicians are centered in San Juan, Ponce, and Mayaguez. Hospital costs are slightly lower than in the States, and Medicare and all other Stateside hospitalization policies are honored. Equipped with 24-hour emergency service, the Ashford Memorial Hospital, 1451 Ashford Ave. in Santurce, has many English-speaking staff members. For help in obtaining a physician, call the Medical Association at 725–6969 or check the Yellow Pages of the telephone directory under *Medicos Especilistas.* Either arrive with an adequate supply of any medications you may require, or bring your doctor's prescription with you. Although diseases like malaria which had been a problem in the past have been eliminated, bilharzia, a disease spread by snails carrying the larvae of the schistosoma parasite, is something to watch out for. Although the chances of infection are remote, it's best to be circumspect when bathing in freshwater pools proximate to human habitation.

conduct: The more Spanish you speak the better. Keep in mind that while Puerto Rico is part of the United States, Latin cultural mores prevail here. Men and women alike tend to dress conservatively. If you want to be accepted and respected, dress respectably. Bathing attire is unsuitable on main streets as is revealing female attire. Eighty years of colonialism have had their effect here and you can expect some acrimony along with the hospitality, though once people come to know you, they will accept you.

what to take: Bring as little as possible, i.e. bring what you need. It's easy just to wash clothes in the sink and thus save lugging around a week's laundry. Remember, simple is best. Set your priorities according to your needs. If you're planning on doing an exceptional amount of hiking, for example, hiking boots are a good idea. Otherwise, they're an encumbrance.

WHAT TO TAKE
CHECKLIST

CLOTHING

socks and shoes
underwear
sandals or thongs
T-shirts, shirts (or blouses)
skirts/pants, shorts
swimsuit
hat
light jacket/sweater

TOILETRIES

soap
shampoo
towel, washcloth
toothpaste/toothbrush
comb/brush
prescription medicines
Chapstick/other essential toiletries
insect repellent
suntan lotion/sunscreen
shaving kit
toilet paper
nail clippers
hand lotion
small mirror

OTHER ITEMS

passport
driver's licence
travelers cheques
moneybelt
address book
notebook

pens/pencils
books, maps
watch
camera/film
flashlight/batteries
snorkeling equipment
extra glasses
umbrella/poncho
laundry bag
laundry soap/detergent
matches/lighter
frisbee/sports equipment

HIKING & CAMPING

internal frame pack
daypack/shoulder bag
foam sleeping bag
ripstop tape
tent/tent pegs
canteen
first-aid kit
binoculars
compass
hiking shorts/pants
candles/candle lantern
pocket knife
nylon cord
utensils
camping stove
can opener
food containers
spices, condiments
scrubbing pads
pots, pans
plastic wrap/aluminum foil

With a light pack or bag, you can breeze through from one town to another easily. Confining yourself to carry on luggage also saves waiting at the airport. See the chart for suggestions and eliminate unnecessary items.

theft: This should not be a problem if you're careful. By all means avoid the slum areas of San Juan, don't flash money or possessions around and, in general, keep a low profile.

services and information: Although the pay phone is still 10¢, service is deplorable and it can cost as much to call from one side of the island to the other as it does to call the States. To use a pay phone, wait for a dial tone *before* inserting money. The number for local information (if it's *not* busy!) is 123. For intra-island calls, dial 129; to call outside Puerto RIco, dial 128; for credit card or third-party calls, dial 130. WATS lines (800 numbers) may be reached by dialing 137 first. For information in English, see the Blue Pages in the center of the telephone directory. The island's area code is 809. Postal service is reliable. Have mail sent c/o General Delivery, Old San Juan PR 00902. Tourist information centers are in Old San Juan, Condado, and at the airport. Be sure to pick up a copy of *Que Pasa,* the free monthly guide to Puerto Rico.

shopping: Opening hours vary but stores are generally open from Mon. through Sat. with some stores closing for an hour in the afternoon. Aside from local handicrafts, there isn't much to buy that can't be found cheaper (or the same price) somewhere else. Some of the better buys are at the factory outlets (Farah, Hathaway, etc.) in Old San Juan. Jewelry is also a popular item in stores here but know your prices at home. There's an import tax on photographic equipment and accessories so bring your own. T-shirts make good souvenirs as do local coffee beans (about $3/lb.). Rum is cheap, and no import duties are charged if bringing it to the States, but other imported hard liquor has duties applied. Poultry and mangoes are among the agricultural products prohibited from export to the States. For details, call the quarantine division of the U.S. Department of Agriculture in San Juan at 791–0356 or 753–4363.

PUERTO RICO ITINERARY

If you have 3 days:
Spend one day in Condado, one day in Old San Juan, and one day in El Yunque, Loiza, or exploring.

If you have 5 days:
Spend one day in Condado, one day in Old San Juan, one day in El Yunque or Loiza, and spend a night each in San German, and Ponce.

If you have one week:
Spend one day in Condado, two days in Old San Juan and Bayamon, one day in El Yunque or Loiza, and spend a night each in San German, and Ponce. Or travel to Coamo, Vieques, Culebra, or Utuado.

Places not to be missed if you have time:
See the museums in Old San Juan and visit Loiza, El Yunque, Vieques, Culebra, Coamo (hot springs), Aibonito, Barran-quitas, one of the nature preserves, Ponce, San German, Bo-queron, Utuado (Caguana ceremonial ball court), and Jayuya.

PUERTO RICO TOURISM COMPANY OFFICES

PUERTO RICO
Calle San Justo 301
Old San Juan, PR 00903
(809) 721-2400

NEW YORK
Sperry Rand Building
1290 Sixth Avenue
New York, NY 10104
(212) 541-6630, (800) 223-6530

LOS ANGELES, CALIFORNIA
Suite 248, 3575 West Cahuenga Boulevard
Los Angeles, CA 90068
(213) 874-5991

CHICAGO, ILLINOIS
Suite 902
11 East Adams Street
Chicago, IL 60603
(312) 922-9701

ATLANTA, GEORGIA
Suite 780, 2635 Century Parkway
Atlanta, GA 30345
(404) 521-5284

DALLAS, TEXAS
Suite 108, 2995 LBJ Freeway
Dallas, TX 75234
(214) 243-3737

CANADA
Suite 501, 10 King Street East
Toronto, Ontario M5C 1 C3, Canada
(416) 367-0190

WEST GERMANY
Mendelssohnstrasse 53
6000 Frankfurt am Main, West Germany
(9069) 742550, 742559

SPAIN
144 Paseo de la Castellana
Entresuelo, Madrid 16, Spain
(13) 457-1093, 453-1094

SAN JUAN AND ENVIRONS

Second oldest city in the Americas (after Santo Domingo) and oldest city in the territorial United States, San Juan presents two distinct faces to the world. One is a vast, sprawling collection of towering concrete monoliths, freeways with crazy drivers, and bleak but functional housing projects with attractive murals painted on their sides. If it appears to have grown too fast, it has. The other face is that of Old San Juan, which retains the original flavor of the city—what the rest of the city must have been like before the svelte skyscrapers arrived. San Juan is divided and subdivided into a number of districts, many of which overlap, and it's nearly impossible to say where one stops and another begins. Sprawling Metropolitan San Juan (pop. 1,086,370) reaches out to touch the municipalities of Bayamon, Canovanas, Carolina, Catano, Guayanobo, Loiza, Toa Baja, and Trujillo Alto. More than one-third of all Puerto Ricans live in this concentrated 300-sq-mile area, the economic, political, social, and cultural capital of the island.

arriving by air: All international flights (and some domestic) arrive at Luis Munoz Marin International Airport which is inconveniently located on the easternmost side of town. Moneychangers, banks, coin lockers, bookstores, a rum-tasting bar (open noon–4 PM) and a taciturn tourist information service (9–5:30) are at the airport. If you don't have too much luggage, catch the T1 bus (25¢) which goes from the airport along Ave. Fernandez Juncos to Old San Juan. Be prepared for a wait. Otherwise, there are always plenty of taxis. Be *sure* that they put the meter on! Limousine service, also out front,

costs $1.75 to Old San Juan and $1.50 to Condado. Service is very irregular so it's best to call (791–4745) to find when the next one is running. In order to shield the taxi drivers from competition, the service is one-way only.

getting around: San Juan was originally served by streetcar lines. Although these have disappeared, streetcar stops are still used to identify destinations. Watch for yellow obelisk posts or the upright metal signs (reading *Parada* or *Parada de Guaguas*) which identify bus stops. The old stops are numbered and identified by red pyramid markers on the Rand McNally map of Puerto Rico. Stops identify a specific area rather than a location. For reference purposes, Stop 8 is near Parque Munoz Rivera in Puerto de Tierra; Stop 10 is in Miramar; Stop 18 is near Ave. Roberto H. Todd; Stop 30 is the Fomento building in Hato Rey; and Stop 40 is at the University of Puerto Rico at Rio Piedras. City buses are 25¢ (no transfers) to any location. Service is irregular and ends early in the evening. Bus terminals in Old San Juan are at Ochoa (in the dock area) and at Plaza de Colon. Other terminals are at Rio Piedras, Country Club, Catano, and Bayamon. The most frequented route is outbound on Ave. Ponce de Leon and inbound (towards Old San Juan) on Ave. Fernandez Juncos. For specific information phone the Metropolitan Bus Authority at 767–7979. Another alternative is to ask around about *publicos* which run from Old San Juan through several metropolitan area destinations, including Rio Piedras and Bayamon. Metered taxis charge 80¢ initially with 10¢ for each additional 1/8 mile. Be sure they put down the meter; San Juan taxi drivers are, according to no less an authority than the Tourism Company Executive Director Miguel Domenech, *estafadores* or "thieves". A series of free open-air wheeled trains, manufactured by a California specialty vehicle company, traverse some of the streets of Old San Juan, many of which have been closed to traffic by white roadblocks that look as if they'd been lifted from the tinkertoy set of some gigantic child. These vans are useful for a rest or for getting your orientation, but their tortoise-like pace and strange routes (such as into the parking lot for five to

Old San Juan street

MAJOR SAN JUAN BUS ROUTES

BUS	ROUTE	POINTS OF INTEREST
1. Rio-Piedras San Juan	Old San Juan Puerto de Tierra. Ave. Ponce de Leon Hato Rey Rio Piedras	The Capitol Munoz Rivera Park Fine Arts Center University of Puerto Rico
2. Rio Piedras Calle Loiza San Juan	Old San Juan Puerto de Tierra Condado Ave. Munoz Rivera Rio Peidras	The Capitol Munoz Rivera Park University of Puerto Rico
8. Puerto Nuevo San Juan	Old San Juan Ave. Ponce de Leon Puerto de Tierra Ave. Kennedy Ave. Roosevelt Rio Piedras	Fine Arts Center Puerto de Tierra The Capitol Roberto Clemente Stadium Hiram Bithorn Stadium Plaza Las Americas University of Puerto Rico
14. Roosevelt Baldrich San Juan	Old San Juan Puerto de Tierra Ave. Ponce de Leon Rio Piedras	The Capitol Fine Arts Center University of Puerto Rico
46. Bayamon F. D. Roosevelt San Juan	Old San Juan Puerto de Tierra Ave. Ponce de Leon Ave. Roosevelt Bayamon	The Capitol Munoz Rivera Park Fine Arts Center Plaza Las Americas Caparra Bayamon Central Park
A7. San Juan Condado Pinones	Old San Juan Puerto de Tierra Ave. Ashford Ave. Fernandez Juncos Isla Verde Carr. 37 Boca de Cangrejos	The Capitol Munoz Rivera Park
T1. Country Club Loiza San Juan	Old San Juan Puerto de Tierra Ave. Fernandez Juncos Carr. 37 Isla Verde Country Club	The Capitol Munoz Rivera Park Fine Arts Center
T2. Country Club Rio Piedras Stop 18	Ave. Ponce de Leon Hato Rey Ave. 65th de Infanteria Country Club	Fine Arts Center University of Puerto Rico

ten minutes) make them an inefficient and cumbersome way to get around. A better idea is to use your feet. Assuming you are in halfway decent physical condition, no place in Old San

Juan is too far to walk to: walking is definitely the best way to savor the atmosphere of the place. Indeed, you'd miss many things by getting around any other way. The section on sights which follows is arranged sequentially from El Morro to San Cristobal, allowing the entire old town to be as systematically and thoroughly explored as possible.

OLD SAN JUAN

For the amount of history, culture, and atmosphere that is packed into its seven-square-block area, no place in the territorial U.S. can begin to touch Old San Juan. Perched on the western end of an islet bordered on the N by the Atlantic and on the S and W by a vast bay, the town is connected to the mainland by the historic San Antonio Bridge. When seen from the harbor, the town takes on the appearance of a gigantic amphitheater with the ramparts and castles forming the outer

City fortifications, Old San Juan

walls. Colonial Spain is alive and well here. Brilliantly restored architecture complements what was well-preserved to
begin with. Old San Juan is not a place to hurry through—it
cannot be seen in a day and can barely be appreciated in a
week. Like a cup of the finest Puerto Rican coffee, it must be
savored and sipped slowly. Stroll through the streets and take
in the local color. See men playing dominoes, girls hanging out
on the street corners waiting for marriage, groceries being
hauled up to a second floor balcony with basket and rope. Get
acquainted with the local characters: watch the crippled man
on crutches who suddenly begins to move at top speed as soon
as he is out of the sight of tourists. Or, if you're lucky, you
might see the man who occasionally brings his pet snake out
for a walk, holding it coiled in his hand and startling his unaware friend seated in a cafe. Or you might see the drunk
singing a soliloquy on a streetcorner. With 5,000 residents, the
panorama of people and events is constantly changing. Feed
the pigeons in Parque de las Palomas or take in the view from
the top of El Morro or San Cristobal. With the exception of the
obnoxious police, nobody hassles anybody in Old San Juan.
Enjoy.

history: Founded as a military stronghold in 1510, San Juan
Bautista became a flourishing and attractive settlement by
the end of the 19th century. Although the town lacks an historic hospital, university, or any of the other significant architectural structures found in Santo Domingo, its buildings
nonetheless have a distinctive charm and appeal of their own.
After the American invasion in 1898, Old San Juan deterio-
rated. Most of it became a red light district until 1949, when
the seven-block downtown was declared a historical zone. Beginning in 1955, the Institute of Puerto Rican Culture, under
the highly imaginative leadership of Ricardo Alegria, began
the tremendous task of restoring the old buildings and homes
in this historical area. Restoration of private residences was
encouraged by legislation exempting owners from taxes for
five to ten years on buildings that have been partially or fully
restored, and offering bank loans for restorative work on liberal terms. Rather than becoming a pretentious museum
piece, Old San Juan is a living historical monument where the

past and present intermingle freely. As nothing within the historical zone could be changed without permission from the Institute, it once seemed unlikely that Old San Juan would be subjected to the "modernization" that mars the rest of the metropolitan area. Under the regime of San Juan Mayor Balthasar Corrada, however, things took a turn for the worse in 1988. After instituting both the shuttle buses and barricades as well as the "changing of the guard"—a tradition without historical foundation—the mayor proceeded to tear up five of the city plazas for remodeling. And, in the case of Plaza de Armas, shade trees were leveled by chainsaw at four in the morning—the morning *before* a protest group was scheduled to meet with the mayor's office! In April, with work on Plaza de Armas virtually completed and Plaza de Colon and several other plazas under reconstruction, Governor Hernandez Colon moved to block work underway on Plaza de San Jose in response to a complaint from Institute of Puerto Rican Culture Director Lopez Soba. Now, in case you hadn't guessed, this all went part and parcel with Corrada's plan to be the NPP's candidate for governor in opposition to the PNP's Hernandez Colon. It just goes to show that politics is still the island's national sport. And even the ambience of a vital and vibrant historical area is not sacred. Check the papers and ask around in Old San Juan about current developments.

Sights

El Morro: A road bordered by wind-blown pines leads up to this dramatic structure, the most impressive legacy of the Spanish empire in Puerto Rico. Along with its sister structure in Havana, Brimstone Hill on St. Kitts (British), and Haiti's La Citadelle, El Morro is one of the premier forts in the Caribbean. Invincible from attack by sea during its time, it's now under the administration of the National Park Service. Open daily from 8–6, free admission; free guided tours at 9, 11, 2, 3:30, tel. 724–1974. Enter the small but cool and carpeted museum and see the exhibits. The rooms on the terrace level were used as living quarters. The doors were made of ultrahard

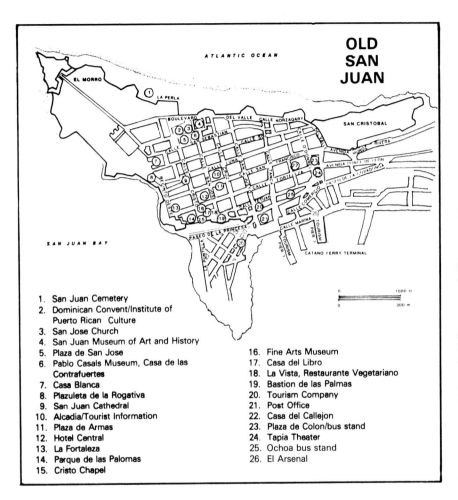

OLD
SAN
JUAN

1. San Juan Cemetery
2. Dominican Convent/Institute of
   Puerto Rican Culture
3. San Jose Church
4. San Juan Museum of Art and History
5. Plaza de San Jose
6. Pablo Casals Museum, Casa de las
   Contrafuertes
7. Casa Blanca
8. Plazuleta de la Rogativa
9. San Juan Cathedral
10. Alcadia/Tourist Information
11. Plaza de Armas
12. Hotel Central
13. La Fortaleza
14. Parque de las Palomas
15. Cristo Chapel

16. Fine Arts Museum
17. Casa del Libro
18. La Vista, Restaurante Vegetariano
19. Bastion de las Palmas
20. Tourism Company
21. Post Office
22. Casa del Callejon
23. Plaza de Colon/bus stand
24. Tapia Theater
25. Ochoa bus stand
26. El Arsenal

ausobo wood, which is now a protected species. See the carefully labeled spots where The Forge, The Kitchen, and The
Latrine (unlabeled) were. The triangular staircase, once an
emergency passage, leads to the gun emplacement. The cannon on the Santa Barbara Bastion, also on the upper level,
were found in the sea. A summer arts festival, including crafts

El Morro

shows, dance groups, and other events, is held yearly from mid-Aug. through the end of Oct. on the fortress grounds.

the fort's history: Built to protect San Juan Harbor, gateway for supply ships headed to Spain's many colonies to the W and S, construction (in 1539) was spurred after recurring attacks by royally commissioned pirates and Carib Indian raids. The site of the fort was moved several times before the present outer fortification was completed in 1584. It was only completed in today's form in 1783, 199 years later, through the efforts of two Irishmen (O'Reilly and O'Daly), by which time about 40,000 man-years had been spent building the fortifications and city walls. Sir Francis Drake, pursuing a cargo of gold pesos being temporarily stored in the fortress' vaults, struck on 22 Nov. 1584, and was repulsed. In 1598 the Earl of Cumberland attacked the Santurce area of San Juan with his 18 ships. Fighting tooth and nail, the Spanish, weakened by dysentery, held out for two weeks before surrendering. Cumberland and his forces were delirious with pleasure until they too succumbed to dysentery, followed by an epidemic of yellow fever. After just four months of control, the English sailed away, leaving 400 of their comrades buried. In 1625, the fortress was attacked by the Dutch, but this time the Spanish survived the attack and began work on San Cristobal on the other side of town, to provide further defense. An attack by British Lt. General Abercromby in 1797 failed (see "La Rogativa" below), and the last attack came during the Spanish-American War, when El Morro's batteries returned fire on U.S. Admiral Sampson's fleet. El Canuelo, which can be seen across the bay, was constructed to ward off hostile landings on the W side. The present structure was rebuilt in stone in the 1660s. Since 1977 $33 million has been spent on repairs to the fortress, including filling in cavities gouged by the sea under the Santa Elena bastion and under the north wall. A 750-foot-long breakwater, constructed by Pennsylvania's Maitland Construction Company at a cost of $7.88 million, is scheduled for completion in October 1990. About 176,060 tons of stone are being used in its construction.

Cemeterio de San Juan: Dramatically situated below towering El Morro, this cemetery contains the graves of such prominent Puerto Ricans as Pedro Albizu Campos and Jose de Diego. The circular neoclassic chapel, dedicated in 1863, is a most unusual architectural edifice. Note its eerie stained-glass reflection. Full-size weeping widows, realistically cut from marble, stand and kneel over graves. Long rows of tombs are set into the wall Etruscan-style, while faded and frayed Puerto Rican flags fly over graves. As space is at a premium, the grave of a less distinguished relative may be dug up and the bones transferred in order to make way for a new arrival. Legendary *independentista* Pedro Albizu-Campos is interred here. Worth a visit, but stay clear at night or risk finding a knife at your throat.

La Perla: Elegant by comparison to the slums which line the banks of the Martin Pena Channel, this slum, situated along the Atlantic to one side of Cemeterio de San Juan, is a crowded group of houses which stretch from just below the remains of the colonial wall down a steep slope to the filthy beach below. Most houses have TVs and other conveniences, and the better part of the slum is served by electricity, water and sanitation service. The area is a center for drug trade and other activities; it is recommended that you not come here unless it's with a local you trust. Bring nothing of value. La Perla is the place where Oscar Lewis penned his study of prostitution and poverty, *La Vida.*

Casa Blanca: One of the gems of Old San Juan. Entering through the gates at 1 San Sebastian, a cool courtyard with a garden and beautiful chain of fountains is off to the left. Straight ahead is a house which has been restored to resemble a 17th C. nobleman's home, with simple but beautifully designed antique furniture and attractive white rooms. Even older than La Fortaleza, this house was designed to be given to Ponce de Leon as a reward for his services. Ponce, however, went off to search for the fountain of youth in Florida and, meeting his end from an Indian's poisoned arrow, never returned. A hurricane destroyed the original structure, which was replaced by another in 1523—which still stands today and has been incorporated into the original structure. In 1779, after more than 250 years residence, Ponce de Leon's descendants sold to the government, which expanded it for use in

La Perla

housing military engineers, and troops. Taken over by the U.S. military in 1898, it was vacated in 1967 and declared a National Historical Monument the following year. A library (open Mon. to Fri. 9-6) has a superb collection of Caribbean literature in Spanish and English. The complex is open Tues. to Sun. 9-12, 1-4:30. Guided tours are available Tues. to Sat.; tel. 724-4102.

El Convento Dominicano: At Calle Norzagaray 98, dominating Plaza San Jose, is the former Dominican Convent, now
headquarters for the Instituto de Cultura Puertorriquena, the
organization responsible for the restoration of Old San Juan.
Built in 1523 on land donated by Ponce de Leon, it's one of the
major historical buildings in the city. After the closure of all
convents in 1838, it was converted to a barracks. After the
American occupation, it was the center of the U.S. Antilles
Command until its termination in 1966. Carefully restored, it
is now a showcase for many fine exhibits of art and antiques,
and cultural events. The restored chapel has old music sheets
complemented by piped-in music, old medals, and the altar-
piece of St. Thomas Aquinas. Concerts are held on occasion in
the huge paved courtyard which lies below the beautiful ar-
caded galleries lined with carved wooden railings. Centro de
Artes Populares is a crafts shop on the ground floor (open
daily, 8–4:30; tel. 724–0700).

El Convento Dominicano, Old San Juan

Museo de Arte y Historie: This former marketplace, located on Calle Norzagay (corner MacCarthur) was restored by the City of San Juan in 1979; it now serves as a cultural center which holds periodic exhibitions, audio-visual displays, and occasional concerts. Open Mon. to Fri., 9–12, 1–5; audio-visual shows Friday at 1 or by prior arrangement for groups, $1 suggested donation, tel. 724–1875.

Iglesia de San Jose: Oldest church still in use in the Americas, San Jose Church was originally built by Dominican friars as a monastery chapel. Originally dedicated to St. Thomas Aquinas, it was renamed by Jesuits who took it over in 1865. The Gothic ceilings are unequaled in this hemisphere. Inside, a statue of Jesus Christ, bleeding and bound with ropes, stands in one corner. This church is most famous for what is missing or moved; most of the items currently on display have been donated. Ponce de Leon's tomb, after a three-and-a-half-century rest, was moved to the cathedral. His coat of arms can still be seen to the left of the main altar. The famous Flemish masterpiece, "The Virgin of Bethlehem," brought to the island in 1511, was stolen (and presumably deflowered) in 1972. During the 1898 U.S. Navy bombardment, a cannonball crashed into one window and mysteriously disappeared; the chapel, crypt, and convent remained untouched. Open Mon. to Fri. 10–4, Sun 11:30–4. Mass is celebrated Sun. at noon.

Museo de Casals: This collection of memorabilia includes cellist Pablo Casals' medals, sweater, cello, domino set, a yellow plaster of Paris cast of his hands, and even his pipes—including one carved in the shape of Wagner! It also holds manuscripts, photographs, and an extensive videotape library (played on request). Open Tues. to Sat. 9:30–5; Sun., 12–5; tel. 723–9185.

Casa de los Contrafuertes; Museo del Grabado Latinamericano: Directly on Plaza San Jose at Calle San Sebastian, next-door to the Museo de Casals, this may be the oldest private residence remaining in Old San Juan. The Casa was constructed in the early 18th C; the name means "heavily-buttressed." Inside, a pharmacy museum is on the first floor. A reconstructed 19th-C. shop is filled with antique crystal and porcelain jars and bottles, mysterious vials, antique medicine ads, as well as other furnishings and objects characteristic of Puerto Rican pharmacies of the time. The Latin American Graphic Arts Museum, which occupies the second floor, contains a superb representative collection of Puerto Rican artists past and present. Particularly notable are the collection of works by Latin American engravers, along with the collection of prized works from the San Juan Biennial. Open Wed. to Sun., 9–12, 1–4:30, tel. 724–5949.

Plaza de San Jose: Restored to its original condition by the Institute for Puerto Rican Culture and reconditioned during 1988, the Plaza is quiet and peaceful and was the liveliest place in town during the night until the Cardinal (who doesn't even live there) complained about the noise. The statue of Ponce de Leon, first governor of Puerto Rico, was cast using melted bronze cannon captured in the 1797 British attack.

Plazuleta de la Rogativa: Designed and built by an Australian residing in Puerto Rico, this remarkable statue, which has a touching spiritual character to it, is located in a small plaza next to the sea wall near Caleta Las Monjas. It was donated by a citizen's group to mark San Juan's 450th birthday in 1971. The statue commemorates a legend concerning the siege of San Juan in 1797. After taking Trinidad on 17 Feb. of that year, Lt. General Abercromby proceeded to San Juan with 60 ships containing nearly 8,000 troops. With the British apparently preparing to close in for the kill, the governor, weakened by dysentery, asked the head bishop to arrange a rogativa ("procession") through the streets. The bishop, in turn, asked that it be held in honor of Santa Catalina (St. Catherine) and Ursula. The evening candle and torch procession moved from Cathedral de San Bautista through the streets. Abercromby became alarmed when he saw the huge masses of torchlights and heard the frenzied continual ring of church bells that increased in tempo until midnight, despite the steady barrage from his ships. Concluding that the town was being supplied by troops from the countryside, he ordered the fleet to sail immediately, which gave rise to the legend that the city had been saved by Ursula and her cohorts.

La Fortaleza: At the end of Calle Fortaleza stands the oldest executive mansion in the Western Hemisphere; it was in operation three centuries before the Washington White House had even been designed. Its name, meaning "The Fortress," derives from its original use. Though replaced by El Morro, it continued to serve as part of the city's defense system. The $2 million in gold and silver which Sir Francis Drake sought during his 1595 attack was kept here. Occupied twice (by the Dutch in 1625 and the British in 1898), it had to be rebuilt in 1640 after the Dutch left. Usage as governor's mansion dates from 1639, and continues today. It was completely remodeled in 1846. Pass by the brusque, rude security guards to join a guided tour of the downstairs area. Open Mon. to Fri.; inquire at tel. 721–7000, ext. 2211, 2358, concerning tour times. Inside, visit Santa Catalina's chapel, descend into the dungeon, and note the Moorish garden with its 19th C. parish tiles. If you stick your hand in the water, you will be granted any wish you request.

San Juan Gate: First of the three city gates built and the sole one remaining. Once the main gate for dignitaries and cargo entering the city, it now serves only to ornament the roadway which passes through it. During the 17th C. sloops anchored in the small cove just N of La Fortaleza. New bishops and governors, entering the city through this gate, would be escorted under a canopy to the cathedral where a Te Deum Mass would be offered in thanksgiving for the safely completed voyage.

Catedral de San Juan Bautista: This is on Calle Cristo across from Plazuleta de las Monjas and El Convento Hotel. Once a small, thatched-roof structure when constructed in 1521, the present cathedral was completed in its present state in 1852. The only holdovers from the earlier structure are the partially restored Gothic ceiling and the circular staircase. See the remains of that ardent Catholic Ponce de Leon, who rests in a marble tomb. The wax-covered mummy of St. Pio, a Roman martyr who was persecuted and killed for his belief in

La Forteleza

Christianity, is encased in a glass box. He has been here since 1862. To his right is a wooden replica of Mary with four swords stuck in her bosom. Many, many beautiful stained glass windows are here. Open daily, 6:30-5. At 51 Caleta de San Juan nearby stands a memorial to a living saint, Felisa Rincon de Gautier, once Mayor of San Juan (1946-68). The former home

San Juan Cathedral

of this pompadoured dynamo has been turned into a small museum. Open Mon. to Friday, 9–4.

Provincial Deputation Building: Recently restored and once occupied by the island's first insular parliament, its cloister-like design is done up in late neoclassical style. Puerto Rico's first representative body, the Provincial Deputation, was housed here. That body began doing business on 17 July 1898, after Puerto Rico was granted autonomy by Spain. The U.S. invaded only two weeks later. It seems appropriate that the building's current occupant is the U.S. Department of State. Open Mon. to Fri. 8–12, 1–4:30; tel. 722–2121.

Plaza de Armas: Relaxed square with pay telephones, supermarkets, small cafeterias, a fruit vendor, and a shaved ice cart. The four statues presiding over the plaza, representing the four seasons, are over a century old. This oblong square has an interesting history. Originally a marketplace (Plaza de las Verduras or Plaza of the Vegetables), it was designed to be the main plaza before Ponce de Leon moved the capital from Caparra. Used during the 16th C. for military drills by local militia, it was also the center of local nightlife. Bands played and singles walked around the square or sat in rented chairs. When the locals were replaced by Spanish garrisons, their cry of "Present arms!" resulted in a name change to Plaza de Armas. It went through several name changes before the name reverted to the present one a few decades ago. Remodeled in 1988 under the administration of San Juan Mayor Baltasar Corrada, it is now so spanking new that it has lost much of its ambience. The shade trees which once graced the plaza were felled in a misguided attempt by the architect to restore the plaza to what it was in the beginning of the century. Two recently restored historical landmarks are right on the plaza: The Intendancy Building, located on the corner of San Jose and San Francisco, was once the offices of the royal Spanish Exchequer. It now houses Puerto Rico's State Department (tel. 722–2121). The Provincial Deputation building once housed the island's first representative body, one which operated for a total of 11 days before the Americans invaded. Both are open Mon. to Fri. 8–12:00, 1–4:30.

Alcadia: Right on Plaza de Armas. Construction on this building, designed along the lines of its counterpart in Madrid, began in 1602. Built in stages, it was completed in 1799. During the years when it functioned as a city hall, many important events took place here, including the inauguration of the first Puerto Rican legislature, and the signing and ratification of the decree abolishing slavery. The last restoration was in 1975. A tourist information center is on the ground floor (formerly a jail) next to a small gallery which holds frequent exhibitions. Open Mon.–Fri., 9–4; tel. 724–7171, ext. 2391.

Museo de Bellas Artes: Located at 253 Cristo St., this small but rich collection of Puerto Rican art is housed in a tastefully restored 18th C. building donated by local citizens. In addition to temporary exhibitions by local artists, there's a permanent collection of artists like Oller and Campeche. Open Tues. to Sun. 9–12, 1–4:30; tel. 723–2320.

La Casa del Libro: This museum of rare books and illuminated manuscripts, housed in a beautifully restored 18th C. townhouse, opened in 1958. Its 5,000-book collection, said to be the best of its kind in Latin America, includes over 2,000 books that date back to the 16th C., and manuscripts dating back 2,000 years. Other books are reference works on the graphic arts. Conveniently located at 255 Calle Cristo. Open Mon. to Fri. (except holidays) 11–4:30.

La Capilla del Cristo: At the foot of Cristo St. stands what must be the smallest chapel in the Caribbean. Dedicated to the Christ of Miracles, there are at least two stories explaining its origin. One claims that it was originally just an altar which prevented people from accidentally falling over the wall into the sea. The other story is more involved. On 24 June 1753, a rider, participating in the annual patron saint festival, missed the turn at the end of Calle Cristo and plunged into the sea. Miraculously, he was not injured, and the chapel was constructed to commemorate the event. In 1925 the city government planned to demolish the chapel, but after vehement public protest, the idea was abandoned. On 6 Aug. every year, the chapel's feast day, the Cardinal of Puerto Rico officiates at a High Mass. Open Tues. 10–4.

Parque de las Palomas: At the end of Cristo St., next to Cristo Chapel, is this small gem of a park, perched at the top of the city wall—nice place to sit early in the morning. Hundreds of pigeons circulate between nook, tree, and fountain. Feathers fly about everywhere. A man sells birdseed at the entrance.

Bastion de las Palmas: Originally constructed in 1678 as a a gun emplacement, it once served as an integral part of the city's defense system. Now it's a small park overlooking San Juan Bay. Grab some morning caffeine at the coffee shop on San Jose and come here for the view. The statue off to the side is of Venezuelan patriot, Gen. Miranda, comrade in arms of Bolivar against the Spanish. His liberal views led to his internment here.

El Arsenal: Built in 1800, this former naval station was the last place in Puerto Rico to be handed over after the 1898 U.S. takeover. Here, the Spanish general waited for the ship which would return him and his men to Spain. Exhibitions are held here. Open Wed. to Sun. 9–12, 1–4. Tel. 724–5949.

Casa del Callejon: This 18th C. home, opened after restoration in 1965, houses the Museo de Arquitectura Colonial, along with the Museo de la Familia Puertorriquena. Downstairs are tiles, blueprints, fittings, and scale models of buildings restored under the auspices of the Institute of Puerto Rican Culture. A good introduction to Old San Juan. Exhibits upstairs show how the rich lived in Puerto Rico during the 19th century. Open Tues. to Sun. 9–12, 1–4; tel. 725–5250. Check out the artisan's market, along the same street (Callejon de la Capilla) on Sat. mornings.

Plaza de Colon: Once much larger, this was formerly named Plaza de Santiago after the gate of the same name. In 1893, to mark the 400th anniversary of Columbus' discovery of Puerto Rico, the plaza was renamed and a statue of the explorer was unveiled. Ponce de Leon's statue was then moved to Plaza San Jose. It was renovated in 1988. Nowadays, it's chiefly of interest for nearby Tapia Theater, Burger King, the largest liquor store in Old San Juan, and its bus terminal.

The Devil's Sentry Box, San Cristobal

San Cristobal: A strategic masterpiece, this imposing fortress, which in its prime covered 27 acres and contained seven
independent but interlocking units, still dominates the E side
of town. Though much smaller now than its more famous
cousin El Morro, it has a less touristy atmosphere. It's nice to
spend the morning sitting and relaxing on the upper level fortifications, taking in the view and getting some sun. Enter the

fortress and find the visitor center, a former guardhouse, on the left. The small museum, located across from the administrative offices on the ground floor, has illustrations detailing how the fort was constructed, a scale model of the original fortification, and a collection of life-sized dolls. On the second floor is a series of low, concave arches and barren rooms. Downstairs, the bronze cannon on an artillery mount was brought down from Delaware while the iron cannons, which deteriorate faster in the salt breeze, were taken from the ocean. Five 150,000-gallon cisterns are on the lower level, and another is on the uppermost level. Water was obtained by rope and bucket, and animals were prohibited inside the fort to prevent contamination. Now, the water is emptied into the sea. The statue of Santa Barbara, patron saint of the fort, also on the ground level, was venerated by the soldiers. The red-and-white flag flying from the upper level is the red cross of St. Andrew. In use from the 16th to 18th C., it symbolizes 400 years of Spanish culture in Puerto Rico. The outer walls are caving in due to erosion caused by waves. It will require an estimated $26 million to repair them. Check out the view of the Devil's Sentry Box, built during the 17th C. at ocean level. A sentry posted here disappeared one night, leaving no trace save his armor, weapons, and clothes. He was thought to have been possessed by the devil. In actuality, he had run off with his girlfriend from La Perla, and they were found to be happily settled on a farm near Caguas years later. It's also possible to see whales migrating from this viewpoint from Nov. to January.

the fort's history: After El Morro proved unable to defend the city, construction began on San Cristobal in 1634 and continued for the next 150 years. The basic structure, however, had been completed and joined to the city walls by 1678. Like El Morro, it was built entirely with materials gathered from the shoreline. Irishmen O'Reilly and O'Day enlisted in the Spanish army and developed ideas for its construction. Incorporating the most advanced ideas of the time, the complex contained six small forts supporting a central core. These are interconnected via an amazingly complex arrangement of passageways, moats, tunnels, bridges, roads, ramps, and dungeons. To storm the central fortress, the enemy would have to take over the six outer forts under continuous fire. Explosives placed under the moats could be ignited if the enemy gained control. In 1898, San Cristobal aimed its guns at an American Naval force, firing the first round in the Spanish-American War. After the American occupation, the U.S. Army moved into the fort. In 1949 it was placed under the National Park Service and opened to the public in 1961. Currently, a feud continues between the NPS and the Commonwealth government. The government's Civil Defense agency was granted part of the fort in 1966, and its lease expired in 1986. However, the agency has refused to move nor to remove the ugly radio antenna and other changes it has made to the fort. The government insists that the agency continue to operate within the fort. It also wishes to convert the adjacent "Three King's Hill" into a parking lot—a move the NPS fears might damage the tunnels lying underneath. The Commonwealth is talking of annexing the fort. This is unlikely, both because it would require an act of Congress and because the Commonwealth would be unable to finance the fort's operation. What the government really wants is for the agency to continue using the fort so that it will not lose face. Open daily, 8–5; guided tours at 9:30, 11, 2, 3:30; tel. 724–1974.

Terminal Turismo: See tour boats come in at Old San Juan's Terminal Turismo. Take a stroll at night while the ships are in and see the tourists. The taxis outside whisk them off to Condado, depriving them of the opportunity to sample San Juan's wonderful nightlife. Across the street is Plazoleta el Puerto, a commercialized and expensive municipal crafts center. Inside the Tourism Pier is the small Museo del Mar (Museum of the Seas) which, in addition to its displays of maritime equipment and models, has wall murals detailing the lifestyle of the Taino Indians.

San Juan Bay and Catano: Reina de la Bahia, a ship holding up to 600 passengers, offers all types of cruises imaginable (evening dinner-dance, disco, student, etc.) for prices ranging from $4–19. Stop by their offices at Pier #6 to pick up a brochure. Another alternative is the cruise ($1.50) which leaves from Pier #2 on Sundays and holidays at 2:30 and 4:30. For a very unusual way to see the bay and its environs try a helicopter tour. The Bell 47J, painted after Eisenhower's helicopter (the first used by the Executive Office), takes off from the roof (10 AM–6 PM) of the Covadonga Parking Lot across from Pier #6 and offers great photo opportunities. Remember that your lens should be no longer than the ASA of your film and that your camera's shutter speed should be set as high as possible to avoid blurring. To make a reservation call Walter or Maria at 724–4585 (789–0881 evenings). Should you drop in, you'll find their young daughter Marcia—who seems to be the one *really* in charge—ready to entertain you with coin games. A more relaxed, leisurely experience is to take the Catano ferry across San Juan Bay to the suburb of Catano. Great views of El Morro and other historic buildings. Board at Pier #2 next to Terminal Turismo in Old San Juan. Ferries leave every half-hour from 5:15 AM to midnight. The fare is 10¢, and the trip is a delight. Bacardi Rum Factory, on the outskirts of Catano, offers free daily tours of its facilities and drinks on the house served under a huge yellow, bat-shaped canopy. It's a long walk to the entrance so take the Levitown bus or a minibus to the entrance. A guard will open the gate; walk straight and then turn right. Orange-and-yellow train-buses carry visitors around the grounds. Although there are regular times posted, tours leave whenever there are sufficient passengers. The guide speaks in a high-pitched, hysterical voice. She may be tipsy or just bored. Visit the distillery, the ersatz museum, and other sites. It'll seem more interesting if you take advantage of the free drinks *beforehand.* Bacardi, largest distiller on the island and largest single source of government tax revenue ($200 million yearly), is also the largest polluter; this plant discharges 634,000 gallons of residue daily into San Juan Bay. A crafts fair here, held on the first and second Sundays in Dec., features exhibits and sales by over 200 craftsmen on the grounds. Also in the vicinity of Catano is Cabras Island. Formerly two separate islands, Cabras and Canuelo, they have been connected by a causeway. Here are the ruins of 17th C. Fort Canuelo and the remains of a leper colony. Great place for a picnic. Seafood restaurants at Palo Seco nearby. Punta Salinas Public Beach is alongside Boca Vieja Bay near Levitown.

Practicalities

accommodations: Although Old San Juan is the best place to base yourself for exploring the metropolitan area, there's a dearth of hotels. The El Convento (tel. 723–9020) is the superior of the two available. Worth a visit, even if you aren't staying there, this hotel is a restored 300-year-old Carmelite Convent situated right in the heart of the old town at 100 Cristo on the corner of Caleta de San Juan right across from the Catedral de San Juan. Inside there's a bar-restaurant (live music in the afternoons), swimming pool, jacuzzi, exercise area, and a rooftop terrace with a great view. Most rooms have balconies and double beds with ikat-like canopies. Winter rates are $85–115 s, $95–125 d, $115–145 t; suites are $175. Summer rates are $75–95 s, $85–115 d, and $100–130 t. For reservations call (800)–228–9898. Hotel Central, located at 202 San Jose just down the street from Plaza de Armas, charges $20 s or $24 d. If staying for an extended period, ask around about renting a room or an apartment.

food: The streets are lined with various eating houses and restaurants ranging from the comparatively plush ones lining Cristo to budget eateries on the other side of town. Highly recommended and reasonable is Govinda's, a Restaurante Vegetariano run by a Hare Krishna-ized Puerto Rican family. Natural food dishes like sopa de vegetales, tortillas, spinach and broccoli, lasagna, and a variety of fresh fruit drinks are lovingly dished out by Jayapatni and her family. A good value is the $3.75 combination plate (noon–2:30 Mon. to Friday; Hare Krishna-sponsored free feed Sat. 11:00–1). For honest Puerto Rican home cooking try El Jibarito, Mr. and Mrs. Ruiz's place, at 276 Sol. Tasa de Oro, corner of Tanca and San Justo, serves up rice and beans ($1.25) and other traditional foods. The eateries lining Plaza de Colon are also inexpensive. Higher but not unreasonably priced is La Bombanera, at 259 San Francisco. Delicious and very unique Puerto Rican style food is served cafeteria style from mid-afternoon until late at

Calle de la Luna, Old San Juan

SAN JUAN ACCOMMODATIONS

KEY: S = single, D = double; T = triple; CP = Continental Plan (Breakfast served); B = beach in vicinity; P = pool; C = casino in hotel; GH = guesthouse.

NOTE: Rates are given as a guideline only; price fluctuations can and will occur. Summer season generally runs 4/15–11/15 or 12/15; check with hotel concerned for specifics. Hotel addresses (except Dorado) are completed with "San Juan, Puerto Rico." Area code is 809. Accommodation tax of 6% applies to all listings.

ADDRESS	TELE-PHONE	WINTER			SUMMER			# OF ROOMS	NOTES
		S	D	T	S	D	T		
OLD SAN JUAN									
El Convento, 100 Cristo, Old San Juan	723-9020	85–115	95–125	115–145	75–95	85–115	100–130	100	P
PUERTA DE TIERRA									
Caribe Hilton, Fort San Jeronimo	721-0303	169–265	189–285		102–192	122–212		707	B, P, C
MIRAMAR									
Clarion, 600 Fernandez, Juncos, Miramar	721-4100	125–145	135–155	150	85–100	95–110	110–120	155	P, CP, C
Excelsior, Ponce De Leon, Miramar	721-7400	85–107	97–119	108–130	67–89	78–100	89–111	140	
Miramar, 606 Ponce de Leon, Miramar	722-6239	38–48	48–60	65	32–38	42–48		48	
Olimpo Court, 603 Miramar, Miramar	724-0600	37–46	40–50	51–61	31–44	33–47	39	45	
Toro, 605 Miramar, Miramar	725-5150 725-2647	25–28	30–35		25–28	30–35	44		
CONDADO									
Atlantic Beach, 1 Vendig, Condado	721-6900	40–70	50–80	90	30–43	40–53	50–63	38	B
El Canario, 1317 Ashford, Condado	724-2793 722-3861	60	70		38	48		25	CP, B, GH
El Canario By the Sea, 4 Condado, Condado	722-8640	60	70		50	50		25	CP, B, GH

(continued)

San Juan Accommodations (continued)

ADDRESS	TELE-PHONE	WINTER			SUMMER			# OF ROOMS	NOTES
		S	D	T	S	D	T		
CONDADO (continued)									
Casa Blanca, 57 Caribe, Condado	722-7139	45	55	65	35-45	45-55	50-63	7	CP, B, GH
La Concha, Ashford, Condado	721-6090	127-177	135-185		87-160	95-185		234	B, P
Condado Beach, Ashford, Condado	721-6090	150-210	160-230		100-120	110-130	135-155	251	B, P
Condado Lagoon, 6 Clemenceau, Condado	721-0170	85	95	110	60	70	80	44	P
Condado Plaza, 999 Ashford, Condado	721-1000	185-220	200-235	225-260	125-175	140-190		587	B, P, C
Dutch Inn & Towers, 55 Condado, Condado	721-0810	85-10	90-105		65-70	70-75		44	P
Howard Johnson's, 1369 Ashford, Condado	721-7300	138-161	148-171		96-120	106-130		150	P
Jewel's By the Sea, 1125 Seaview, Condado	725-5313	inquire			35-65			8	B, GH
El Portal, 76 Condado, Condado	721-9010	70-80	85-95		55-65	65-75	75-90	48	CP
El Prado Inn, 1350 Luchetti, Condado	728-5925	50-55	65-70		35-45	45-55		20	CP, B, P, GH
Ramada San Juan, 1045 Ashford, Condado	724-5657	145-175	155-185	185-215	90-130	100-140	120-160	196	B, P, C·
The Regency, 1005 Ashford, Condado	721-0505	100-120	110-125		85-105	85-105		129	B, P
Tamana, 1 Joffre, Condado	724-4160	45	55	65	28-32	38-42	43-48	95	

(continued)

San Juan Accommodations (*continued*)

ADDRESS	TELE-PHONE	WINTER			SUMMER			# OF ROOMS	NOTES
		S	D	T	S	D	T		
SANTURCE									
Bolivar, 609 Bolivar, Santurce	727–3823	20	25	48	23	29	51	40	
Pierre, 105 De Diego, Santurce	721–1200	87	97		66	76		184	P
OCEAN PARK									
Arcade Inn, 8 Taft, Ocean Park	725–0668 728–7524	35–38	45–50		30–35	40–45		19	GH
Beach House, 1957 Italia, Ocean Park	727–4495	45–70	55–80		25–45	35–55		9	CP, B, GH
La Condesa, 2071 Cacique, Ocean Park	727–3968 727–3900	42	48		35	42		15	CP, P, GH
Numero 1 on the Beach, 1 Santa Anna, Ocean Park	727–9687	55–65	75–80		32–38	48–60		7	P, GH
San Antonio, 1 Tapia, Ocean Park	727–3302	39	49		30–60	35–65		7	B, GH
Wind Chimes, 53 Taft, Ocean Park	727–4153	50–70	50–70		30–35	40–45		11	CP, GH
PUNTA LAS MARIAS/ISLA VERDE									
Tres Palmas, 2212 Park, Punta Las Marias	727–4617	55–70	55–70		35–55	35–55		8	B, P, GH
Carib-Inn, Carr. 187, Isla Verde	791–3535	90	95	110	55–80	60–85	75–100	225	B, P
Casa Mathiesen, 14 Uno Este Villamar, Isla Verde	726–8662 727–3223	41–60	48–60		45–50	45–50		18	P, GH
Don Pedro, 4 Rosa, Isla Verde	791–2838	49	57		39	47		16	P
Empress Oceanfront, 2 Amapola, Isla Verde	791–3083	115–125	125–140	140–160	75–95	85–130	100–140	30	B, P

(continued)

San Juan Accommodations (*continued*)

ADDRESS	TELE-PHONE	WINTER			SUMMER			# OF ROOMS	NOTES
		S	D	T	S	D	T		
PUNTA LAS MARIAS/ISLA VERDE (*continued*)									
ESJ Towers, Carr. 37, Isla Verde	791–5151	150	155	185	110	115	145	319	B, P
Green Isle, 36 Uno, Villa-mar	726–4330	41–60	48–60		33–37	37–50		17	B, P, GH
International Airport, 3rd F, Airport Terminal Building, Isla Verde	791–1700	45	50	56	55	60	66	57	
Mario's, 2 Rosa, Isla Verde	791–3748	45	45	50	40	40	45	59	P
Patio, 87 Tres Oeste, Isla Verde	728–9921	40	45	50	38	42	48	14	P, GH
La Playa, 6 Amapola, Isla Verde	791–1115	45	53–63		35	45–53		15	B
Sands, 6 Earle, Isla Verde	724–7272	175–265	185–275	210–300	110–180	120–190	145–215	429	B, P, C
San Juan, Isla Verde	791–1000	185–355	195–365		180–270	190–280		392	B, P, C
DORADO									
Hyatt Regency Cerromar, Carr. 693, km 11.8, Dorado	796–1010	200–275	275–440		95–145	95–145		508	CP, B, P
Hyatt Dorado Beach, Carr. 693, Km 10.8, Dorado	796–1600	275–440	275–440		110–190	150–230		308	CP, B, P

night at Krugger's, 52 San Jose close to Plaza San Jose. Food ranges from pastries to full meals. Joseph's Cafe, 206 San Francisco, is just down the street. La Danza, corner Fortaleza and Cristo, has a $12 paella special for two which includes coffee, pastry, salad, and a small bottle of wine. **formal food:** More expensive are Patio de Sam and Amadeus at Plaza San

Jose. Zaragozana is at 356 San Francisco. Danza is at 56 Fortaleza. Others include Frailes and Patio de Convento inside
the El Convento at 100 Cristo; Galanes at 65 San Francisco
(inside an attractively restored house); Farol at 411 San Francisco; Tetuan 20 at 255 Tetuan; La Vista at 151 Tetuan;
Chaumiere at 367 Tetuan; Mauriccio's at 309 Recinto Sur;
Tango's at 313 Recinto Sur; Meson Vasco at 47 Cristo; Mago's
Steak House at 257 Tanca; Mallorquina at 207 San Justo;
Nuevo Cafeteria de San Juan at 152 Cruz; Butterfly People at
152 Fortaleza; and Cafe de Puerto (only open to non-members
for lunch) is at Plazoleta del Puerta near the cruise ships, as is
La Isla Bonita. **fast food:** Fast-food freaks can find relief at an
unusually aesthetic Burger King (complete with waterfall),
right on Plaza Salvador Brau, and a spacious Taco Maker at
255 San Justo. Baldwin's Victoria Oven Baked Potato ($1.95
w/cheddar, chili, or chicken) carts are found near the tourist
information on Calle Comercio. Pizza Hut, McDonalds, and
Baskin Robbins line Calle Fortaleza. Ponderosa is at Tetuan
and San Justo. **snacks, sandwiches, and drinks:** Just
around the corner from Calle Tetuan on Calle San Jose, Cafeteria Los Amigos has the cheapest morning coffee in town
along with sandwiches. Various signs posted include "no dis-
cuta politica." El Escenario, 152 Calle San Sebastian, has
sandwiches and 50¢ coffee in ceramic cups (instead of the ubiquitous paper), and about the only herbal tea in town. Maria's,
204 Calle Cristo, is famous for its delicious but pricey (around
$2.50) fresh frozen fruit drinks. Asti's, across the street, has
pizza slices ($1.25) as well as other Italian food. A *heladeria* on
Plaza San Jose has *batidas* (shakes) for $1.10 and cones for
65¢.

entertainment: For its size, Old San Juan has a greater con-
centration and more variety of nightlife than anyplace else in
the United States. Cobblestone-lined streets are packed wall to
wall with nightspots ranging from sleaze bars to elite discos.
Its dynamic and unmistakably Latin environment gets wild at
night—especially on weekends when cars pour in. Everyone is
desperate to see and be seen in this modern version of the
paseo, the traditional evening along the plaza. Well-heeled
couples promenade up and down Calle Cristo. Fashionable

clothes and tons of makeup are everywhere in evidence—
everyone heading up to the bar-lined streets surrounding the
Plaza San Jose. On the Plaza, in addition to the young middle-
class bar scene, there are often jams with congo bands or folk
musicians. It has gotten so wild up here at times that the
police have come by and fired shots into the air. One balcony
overhanging the plaza still has bullet holes. Plenty of action
and atmosphere in the surrounding streets as well. Innumerable bars, scattered throughout the town, have pool tables, TVs,
and pinball machines. Here you can drink a beer for as little
as 65¢.

information: Check the "Performance" section of the Thurs-
day *San Juan Star's* "Entertainment Guide" to find out
what's going on. *Que Pasa* also has listings. And the excellent
(Spanish only) *Calendario* put out by the Institute of Puerto
Rican Culture and available at their offices inside the Dominican Convent on Plaza San Jose, gives information on local
events. Another way is to check for posters. **music and theater:** As good a place as any to start an evening—or finish one
for that matter—is El Escenario at 152 San Sebastian. Run by
members of an international organization concerned with
world ecology, this attractive venue often has theater and musical performances on weekends. The Place at 154 Fortaleza
has excellent jazz bands in a spacious setting. No cover jam
sessions run Mon. to Wed. from 10 PM. Tony's, an extremely
attractive cafe at 273 San Sebastian, has soft Latin jazz (and
sometimes rock) on weekends from 9:30. No cover ($5) is
charged if you arrive before the band starts. Cafe La Violeta,
56 Fortaleza, features a dark, romantic environment that
seems expressly designed for romantic tete-a-tetes. A pianist
plays Thurs. to Sat. from 9–2 AM. Tetuan 20, 255 Tetuan, features live guitar music Thurs. and Fri. evenings. Pianists perform nightly (10–3 AM) at Cafe Alejandro, on O'Donnel
between Fortaleza and Tetuan. For formal theater, try the Tapia. **bars:** Expatriates hang out at PJ's on San Jose. Farther
up San Jose is El Batey, another Americano hangout, which is
open "until the last cat goes home." At 52 San Jose near the
top of the street is Krugger's, run by fanciful Friquitin Krugger, an emigre from Mayaguez. Note the outstanding stained

glass work above the bar by local artist Lance Bon (and check out what one of the elephants is doing!). The magnificent block print in the back is by Roberto Rodriguez who lives next door. Cafe De Abufio serves every coffee and coffee drink you can imagine and then some. It overlooks Plaza de Armas. **discos:** Lazer Videoteque is at 251 Cruz and Neon's Videoteque is at 203 Tanca (Wed. to Sat. from 10 PM). Both cater to a very decked out, youthful crowd, including cruise ship passengers with vouchers. **cinema:** Good value for films is the theater at Calle San Justo 154. Double features are just $2.50.

events and festivals: Most of the island-wide festivities find their fullest expression here. A Puppet Theater Festival is held in Jan., as is an international folklore festival and the San Sebastian Street Fiesta; this popular street fair has everything from processions and dancing in the plaza to displays of Paso Fino horses. Streets are absolutely packed. The Festival de Claridad (Festival of Clarity) takes place in Feb. The Festival de Teatro Puertorriqueno (Festival of the Puerto Rican Theater) is held at the Tapia Theater each March. While the Fiesta de la Musical Puertorriquena is held inside the Dominican Convent each May; the Festival de Verano (Summer Festival) and the Casals Festival (which attracts the top names in classical music) are in June. Centering on 26 June, San Juan's most famous fiesta, dedicated to San Juan Bautista, is celebrated as inhabitants (including the mayor) flock to the sea for the traditional midnight dip which is believed to wash away sin. A ceramics fair takes place each August. These events are subject to change so check the latest issue of *Que Pasa* to find out what, indeed, is happening. And, again, the *Calendario* of the Institute of Puerto Rican Culture is a good source.

crafts and shopping: Don't expect to find any great bargains here. What you will find, among the kitsch, are some good buys. Probably the best of these is clothing. Factory outlets sell discounted clothes made on the island. The Farah Factory Outlet is at Valu, 208 San Francisco. London Fog Factory Outlet Store is at 156 Cristo. Hathaway Factor Outlet is at 203 Cristo. The Bass Shoe Factory Outlet is at 206 Calle Cristo. Barrachina, Calle San Francisco, has free rum samples. Butterflies by Rose has beautiful plexiglass boxed butterflies (mostly from Brazil, Peru, and Africa). It's located next to Hotel Central at 202 San Jose. Galeria Penelope, 107 San Sebastian, contains the island's first and only collection of "wearable art." It features women's dresses, men's hand painted "salsa" tee shirts, etc. A small art gallery is adjacent. The Folk Art Center, inside the Dominican Convent on Plaza San Jose, has an excellent selection of island handicrafts—buy here and help support a worthy cause. Jose E. Alegria's handsome shop at 154 Cristo houses a fascinating collection of *santos* and pre-Columbian artifacts. See men hand-rolling cigars at a shop inside the Ochoa bus depot. **jewelry stores:** These include London House at 206 San Jose; Rainbow Jewelry at 105 Fortaleza; Maximo, 250 San Francisco; Faro, 357 Fortaleza; Gitana, 304 Fortaleza; Catala, at Plaza de Armas; Corsalina, 350 San Francisco; Ramon Lopez, 256 Fortaleza; One Stop Shopping, 302 San Francisco; Nayor, 250 San Francisco; Yas Mar, 205 Fortaleza; Boveda, 209 Cristo; and Demel, 261 Fortaleza. **art galleries:** Puerto Rican artists are well represented in Old San Juan's many galleries. In addition to the exhibits held inside Casablanca, La Arsenal, the Alcaldia, and the Museo de Arte y Historia, there are a number of private galleries: Galeria Botello, which displays the works of the Spanish expatriate namesake as well as other artists, is at 208 Cristo. Galeria Luigi Marrozzini is at 156 Cristo. Galeria M.S.A. is at 266 San Francisco. Galeria San Juan is on Norzagaray at the corner of San Justo. The San Juan Art Students League holds exhibits in a blue building in front of Iglesia San Jose.

information and services: Minimal tourist information is provided in offices in the Alcadia (City Hall) on Plaza de Armas (tel. 724–7171), at 301 San Justo (tel. 721–2400), and at La Casita, a renovated building near the post office. Pharmacies are located on the Plaza de Armas and at the corner of Luna and Cruz. Newspapers (including *The New York Times*) are found at the former as well as near the post office. For changing money and cashing traveler's checks, the Bank of Nova Scotia, 251 Tetuan, and the Royal Bank of Canada, 204 Tetuan, are open Mon. to Fri. from 9–2:30. The Bookstore, which is an excellent bookstore, is located near the corner of

San Jose and Tetuan. An a/c library is located inside Casa Blanca. A post office is located at the corner of Recinto Sur and San Justo; pick up mail addressed c/o General Delivery, Old San Juan 00905 (most convenient location in the city). Passport photos can be taken at Fortaleza 65. A laundromat is located at corner of Cruz and Sol.

METROPOLITAN SAN JUAN

Puerto De Tierra

Literally named "Land at the Door," this compact area, once right outside the old city walls, was originally settled by freed black slaves. Nowadays, Puerto de Tierra contains numerous U.S. Naval Reserves, the Capitol, and other governmental buildings. Avenida Ponce de Leon runs right through its center.

Capitol, Puerto de Tierra

sights: Seat of the Puerto Rican bicameral legislature, the Capitol was constructed during the 1920s. Its magnificent dome, with its coat of arms, hangs over an urn displaying the 1952 constitution. Open Mon. to Fri. 8:30–5. For guided tours, call 721–6040, ext. 253. The once exclusive Casino de San Juan, constructed in 1917, has since been renamed the Manuel David Fernandez Government Center and converted to use by the State Department. Recently restored with marble floors and walls and a 12-foot chandelier (open Mon. to Fri., 8–4:30; tel. 722–2121). A statue of patron saint San Juan Bautista, across from the Capitol and overlooking the small beach below, bears an uncanny resemblance to Mr. Natural, of underground comic book fame. Gracefully landscaped Munoz Rivera Park contains a statue of its namesake which stands near El Polvorin, an ammunition depot and small museum. Eighteenth-century Fort San Geronimo, entered from the rear of the Caribe Hilton, houses a museum featuring dummies

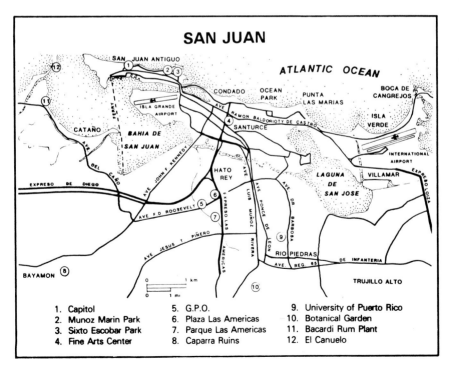

1. Capitol	5. G.P.O.	9. University of Puerto Rico
2. Munoz Marin Park	6. Plaza Las Americas	10. Botanical Garden
3. Sixto Escobar Park	7. Parque Las Americas	11. Bacardi Rum Plant
4. Fine Arts Center	8. Caparra Ruins	12. El Canuelo

wearing military uniforms of different eras, ship models, and other war material. Open Wed. to Sunday, 9–12, 1–4:30; tel. 724–5949.

accommodations: Least expensive is Hotel Ocean Side, 54 Munoz Rivera (tel. 722–2410). On the upper end is the Caribe Hilton: the island's oldest resort hotel. Its oldest building dates from 1849. At one time visitors to the island came here directly from the airport and (aside from time spent shopping in Old San Juan), the hotel environs were as much of the island as they saw! (See "Accommodations Chart")

food: Preeminent place (and one you won't want to miss) is El Roble. With a deli out front and a restaurant in the back, here you can find an assortment of everything from beer and cheese to Cuban cigars from Miami. El Amendro nougats from Spain are a delicacy as are *durrones*, the locally produced Christmas candies. Try to grab a slice of cheesecake after it comes out fresh from the oven. For an expensive $9 an entire can of peaches imported from Spain can be yours. Try *quesito*, a tasty cheese pastry. Pancho Romano and the *empanadas* (meat pies) are also recommended. Other restaurants include Ponce de Leon pizza parlor, Restaurant La Imperial (another deli), Hao Hao (Chinese fast food and ice cream)—all along Ponce de Leon. More expensive are the Tasca at 54 Munoz Rivera, the Cathay at 410 Ponce de Leon, and the Rotisserie inside the Caribe Hilton.

shopping: Buy handicrafts at Mercado de Artesania Puertorriquena inside Munoz Riviera Park and at Mercado Artesania Carabali, Sixto Escobar Park. The former is open only on Sunday. A number of small shops line Ponce de Leon.

services: A postal station is located along Ponce de Leon. The Archives and General Library, at 500 Ponce de Leon, has served as a library, cigar factory, and rum plant. It displays books and archives from the collection of the Institute of Puerto Rican Culture. Its small chapel might seem to be an unusual feature but keep in mind that it was originally designed as a hospital. Open Mon. to Friday, 8–5. Also try the small library inside the ornate Biblioteca Ateneo Puertorriqueno, Ave. Ponce de Leon.

Miramar

This is a high-class residential area just across the bridge from Puerto de Tierra. The many beautiful homes here include several by architect Antonin Nechodoma, whose work shows the marked influence of Frank Lloyd Wright. Yachts shelter at Club Nautico on the bay side of the bridge Isla Grande, just beside Miramar to the W. It was formerly a U.S. Naval base and is now the site of Isla Grande Airport (domestic). A large number of birds can be seen in this area.

accommodation: A good accommodation value at 605 Miramar is the Hotel Toro (tel. 725–5150) with friendly and helpful management (by Mr. and Mrs. Toro of course), lounges, and sundeck. Year round rates start at $20 s and $28 d. More expensive rooms have a/c and/or kitchenettes. Nearby are the Miramar, Olimpo Court, Excelsior, and Clarion hotels.

food: Ponce de Leon and surrounding sidestreets are literally lined with places to eat. For sandwiches and expresso try the

Miramar

Panaderia y Repositeria at the corner of Miramar and Ponce de Leon. More expensive bistros include Casa Eusebio inside Club Nautico; Fabada, next to Hotel Olimpo, at 603 Miramar; D'Arco at the base of Hotel Toro, 605 Miramar; Ail-oli, inside the Excelsior, at 801 Ponce de Leon; and the Windows of the Caribbean, atop lofty Hotel Clarion, 600 Fernandez Juncos. Open until 9, the Pueblo Supermarket has the usual stuff including bulk coffee beans.

entertainment: The Fine Arts Cinema, 654 Ponce De Leon, has high quality first run films. Other theaters, including the island's only porn theater, are farther down the road in Santurce. The Clarion Hotel's Windows of the Caribbean restaurant has live entertainment most evenings. The Black Angus is one of the local meat markets. The "hoofers" here have a lower incidence of AIDS (because they force their customers to use condoms) than the street hookers nearby. The Hawaiian Hut down the road (instantly recognizable by its twin totem poles) is a sleazy strip joint.

services: Many airline offices are based in the Miramar area: Iberia, Capitol, Viasa, Mexicana, Lufthansa, Dominicana. The information service center for the Dominican Republic is at Miramar Plaza, 954 Ponce de Leon. The French Consulate is in Edificio Centro de Seguros, Suite 412, Ave. Ponce de Leon 701.

airport: Situated at the end of a long stretch of road near the tractor trailer "Sea Train" terminal sits small and funky Isla Grande, which served as the island's first international airport. Inside are a cafeteria and several airlines including Flamingo, who fly to Culebra, and Vieques Air Link who fly to Vieques and on to St. Croix. Isla Grande Flying School (tel. 722–1180, 725–5760) rents small planes for solo ($60/hr.) and dual ($70/hr.) flying with a three-hour minimum. Fuel, oil, and liability insurance are included. Unfortunately, the only way to get to this airport is via a long, hot walk, your own wheels, or by taxi.

Santurce-Condado

Once the most exclusive area in the city, Santurce is now deteriorating rapidly as businesses move over to the neighboring financial district of Hato Rey. Condado, the tourist strip on the main bus route between Old San Juan and the rest of the city, is as near to a perfect replica of Miami Beach as you'll find in the Caribbean. Check out the scene if you must. If you want to escape from Puerto Rico, this is the place to do it. Avenida Ashford, once famous for its hookers, now hosts male prostitutes and drug pushers. Whatever you do, keep off the beaches at night, or risk a mugging. **history:** Founded as Cangrejos (later San Mateo de Cangrejos), the area was the main agricultural and meat supplier to Old San Juan from the 17th C. onwards. Inhabited mostly by freed slaves and Maroons (refugees from slavery on other islands), its name changed to Santurce. The bridge linking Condado with Puerto de Tierra was constructed originally in 1910 by two brothers (the Behns) who were early 20th C. immigrants from St. Thomas. The name (Dos Hermanos, "Two Brothers") of the current rebuilt and enlarged structure still refers to Hernand and Sosthenes who, after acquiring the Puerto Rican Telephone Company, went on to found ITT! Calle Luchetti is named after their mother, Madame Luchetti. Ave. Ashford's namesake is Dr. Bailey K, Ashford who came to the island with the occupying American troops. He discovered that hookworms are the root cause of anemia. During the turbulent late 1950s in Cuba and after the revolution which followed, Condado was quick to soak up the tourists (and many Cubans) who fled, seeking a more hospitable environment. The area's most unusual "sight" must surely be the Tunel Minillas in Santurce. It's nicknamed the "carwash" because of its leaky roof.

accommodations: Guesthouses include the Prado, Casa Blanca, El Canario, and El Canario by the Sea. More inexpensive are Casa Cervantes, 10 Cervantes (tel. 723–8346) and Hosteria del Mar, 5 Cervantes (tel. 724–8203), and Safari on the Beach, 2 Yardley Place, Ocean Park (tel. 726–0445). Hotels include the Atlantic Beach, the Portal, Tamana, Howard Johnson's, Condado Lagoon, Dutch Inn & Tower, the Regency, the Concha, Condado Beach, Ramada San Juan, and the Condado Plaza. (See accommodations chart for details.) Also try the Hotel Capri, 902 Fernandez Juncos, Santurce (tel. 722–5663); Hotel Colonial, Inc., 1902 Fernandez Juncos, Santurce (tel. 727–1440); Hotel Dos Hermanos, 263 Duffaut, Santurce (tel. 725–4349); Hotel Lindomar, 4 Condado, Santurce (tel. 724–8640); Hotel Metropol, 1661 Ponce de Leon, Santurce (tel. 723–8080); Hotel Pierre-Best Western, 105 Ave. De Diego, Santurce (tel. 721–1200); Hotel San Jorge, 1700 Ponce de Leon, Santurce (tel. 727–1223), and Simar, 166 Villamil, Santurce (tel. 723–9111).

food: There are innumerable places to eat. For Puerto Rican food try any cafeteria or Criollisimo, 2059 Ave. Edo Conde, Santurce; Restaurant La Borincana, 1401 Fernandez Juncos; and Restaurante El Ateneo, 610 Figueroa. How Kow, 1408 Magdalena, features Cantonese and Szechuan dishes. A converted mansion, Antonio's, 1406 Magdalena, serves Spanish food and seafood. The usual fast food chains are everywhere in evidence: the Burger King here is the most expensive in Puerto Rico. Salud, 1350 Ave. Ashford, a natural health food restaurant and store, serves great food Mon. to Sat., 9–8 PM (tel. 722–0911). In addition, every hotel has its own restaurant. **supermarkets:** Pueblo is at 114 De Diego, Vega's Supermarket is at Hotel Condado Lagoon, 6 Clemenceau, Condado. Santurce Market is on Calle Canals.

entertainment: The Fine Arts Center (tel. 724–4751), largest and best of its kind in the Caribbean, is also the most attractive building in the entire area. Since it opened in 1981, the Center has featured internationally acclaimed musicians, ballet stars, opera and experimental dance performances, lectures, drama festivals, jazz concerts, and musical comedies. Student discounts are available. Be sure to get there early or buy tickets in advance if you want the cheaper seats. Nuestro Teatro presents plays dealing with Puerto Rican life and social realities. Shannan's Irish Pub, 1503 Loiza, Santurce, has the reputation of being the wildest joint in town. The Greenhouse, 1200 Ashford Avenue, has live entertainment from 11 on Wed., Sat., and Sun. nights. Touristic shows are put on regularly at the major hotels in the area; check *Que Pasa* for listings. Gay bars include Bachelor and Topaz. **cinema:** UA Paramount is at 1313 Ponce de Leon, Santurce. Metro is at 1255 Ponce de Leon, Santurce.

services and information: Information about the island is available inside El Centro Convention Center on Ave. Ashford. Located across from the Sheraton at 1300 Ashford, is the information service center for the Virgin Islands. Bell, Book, and Candle, the city's leading bookstore, is at 102 De Diego. Alianza Francesa (Alliance Francaise) is at 206 Rosario, Santurce. They have a library and present films and other cultural events. The Dutch Consulate is at First Federal Savings, Stop #23, Ave. Ponce de Leon.

Hato Rey

Sometimes called "the Golden Mile" or "the Wall Street of the Caribbean," Hato Rey is notable only for its skyscrapers, those lyrical concrete-and-steel paeans to the wonders of capitalist endeavor. The huge federal complex, the offices of Fomento, and the Western Hemisphere overseas operations headquarters of the Chase Manhattan Bank are all located here, as are the gigantic Bancos de Santander and Ponce. Without these, Hato Rey would be nothing more than a desolate, land-filled marsh.

accommodation: Hotel Europa is at 64 Navarro (tel. 763–1524).

restaurants: For Puerto Rican food, Metropolitan Restaurant and Coffee Shop is at Metropolitan Shopping Center. El Chotis Taberna Espanola, 187 O'Neill features Spanish Cuisine. Others include the Asturiana, 191 O'Neill; Chavales, 253 Roosevelt; Costa Brava, 137 Roosevelt; Yuan, 255 Ponce de Leon; and Zipperle, 352 Roosevelt.

services: The General Post Office is on Roosevelt Avenue. Take a no. 8 bus from Plaza Colon, Old San Juan. Plaza Las Americas, a gigantic shopping mall, is a playground for the affluent; free coffee samples are offered downstairs; branches of Galerias Botello and Bell, Book, and Candle (bookstore) are located upstairs, while Thekes Bookstore is on the first floor. A number of restaurants are also located here.

Rio Piedras

This student area of the city has the University of Puerto Rico, the attractive Paseo de Diego (cheaper than the shopping malls), and a great market near the bus terminal. At the center of the campus stands the Roosevelt bell tower. Done up in a gaudy pink, it is Spanish influenced but bears a passing resemblance to a South Indian Tamil Nadu Hindu temple. Theodore Roosevelt donated the money and so received the dubious distinction of having it as his namesake. See the three sculptured heads set in front of the bell tower. The campus has a relaxed, laid-back atmosphere with students playing guitars and petting in the Jose M. Lazaro Library. Largest general library on the island, it contains the Juan Jiminez Room, which displays memorabilia belonging to the famous Spanish expatriate poet. A small but intriguing *museo* next to the library features archaeological artifacts as well as special art exhibitions.

Rio Piedras Market: Located on De Diego Street, its fairly wide aisles are numbered with signs showing which produce is being sold. Packed with fruits (pineapples, papaya, golden-skinned oranges), common and more exotic (*yuca, yautia*) vegetables, and island spices (ginger, mint, cilantro). An arcade section sells clothes. Best time to visit is early morning when merchants and farmers unload trucks and pack booths. Savor the atmosphere.

food: Many cheap places to eat. Esquina Universidad, on the

Roosevelt Tower, University of Puerto Rico

corner of Ponce de Leon and Gandara, is a popular student hangout. The owner here addresses students according to what island town they come from. There's also the usual assortment of fast food places including a Taco Maker at Ponce De Leon 1000. Energy, a health food store and restaurant, is at Ave. Diego #2 (open Mon. to Sat., 9–3; tel. 764–2623). Sun y Cream, at Ponce de Leon 1004, is a cheap Chinese restaurant ($1.25 and up) which also serves ice cream. Tomas Ice Cream, across the street, is an attractive student meeting place. More expensive are Casa Maria, 273 Jesus Pinero, and Kimpo Garden, 264 Jesus Pinero.

entertainment: The Casals Festival takes place on the University of Puerto Rico campus in May. The University also offers a cultural activities series which features ballet and classical music performances and avant-garde films. For information contact Dr. Francis Schwartz, Actividades Culturales, at 764–0000, ext. 2563/2567. Cine Teatro Rio Piedras, in addition to plays and concerts, offers films.

bookstores: Liberia La Tertulia, corner of Amilia Marin and Gonzales, and Libreria Hispanoamericano, 1013 Ponce de Leon, are open Mon. to Saturday. Other bookstores are located in Plaza Las Americas, Hato Rey.

Agricultural Experimental Station: Operated by the University of Puerto Rico, it is still in Rio Piedras but way off in the boonies. Take the no. 19 bus from Ochoa terminal in Old San Juan. Pack a picnic lunch. The Botanical Garden here is open Tues. to Sun. 9–4:30 (tel. 766–0740). There's no admission charge to visit this enchanting area, which includes an orchid garden with exotics like dendrobiums, epidendruns, and vandas and a palm garden featuring 125 species. Broad paths traverse an incredible range of vegetation, from a flaming African tulip tree and croton bushes to endless varieties of palms and ferns. Woody lianas hang from trees. Cool off in one of several libraries and check in the Forest Service office for detailed info about El Yunque's rain forest.

Bayamon

A suburban municipality of San Juan, Bayamon has shifted from being an agricultural to an industrial community. It's still growing extremely fast. More than 200,000 people and some 170 factories make their home here. The city is renowned for its chicharron. This local delicacy (from the Spanish verb *achicharrar* "to smoke") originated when slaves, given the skin torn from pigs by the Spaniards, hung them over the coals to dry. The grease dripped into the fire, and the result was a crisp and curly morsel—now one of the standbys of Latin cuisine. **getting there:** Take bus no. 46 from San Juan or find one of the buses that occasionally run from near the G.P.O. in Old San Juan. Yet another alternative is to take the Catano ferry (10¢) and then a *publico* (40¢).

sights: Just before Bayamon on Carr. 2, km 6.4 at Guayanobo, are the ruins of Caparra, the first colonial settlement on the island. Established by Ponce de Leon in 1508, it was abandoned for the Old San Juan site 12 years later. Only the masonry foundations, uncovered in 1936, remain. To the rear, a small museum contains Taino artifacts and tools, weapons, and tiles found at the site (open Mon. to Fri., 8:30-noon, 1–4:30). Inside the municipality itself, directly across from the City Hall, the immaculately landscaped grounds of Central Park contain a country house, which functions as a small museum, and the only locomotive train remaining in Puerto Rico, which runs through the grounds. This museum also displays artifacts excavated during archaeological digs at the site. Junghanns Park, several blocks to the W, features trees from all over the world which were planted by the local botanist of the same name. Adjacent to Bayamon's plaza and in the heart of the historical zone, the former city hall contains the Museo de Oller, named after the famous local resident realist-impressionist painter (open Tues. to Saturday, 9–4). This recently restored neoclassic building is painted in shades of blue, pink, and yellow—evocative of a San Francisco gingerbread. Inside, the first level has one room dedicated to Francois Oller's portraits of local notables and one room containing indigenous artifacts and a collection of Taino skulls. The remaining rooms are largely devoted to the remarkable artwork of the local artist Tomas Batista. His work includes bronze and fiberglass busts and fossilized stones carved and polished into the shape of gigantic seashells. The top floor contains governorial and mayoral portraits by local artist Tulio Ojedo and a genuine mayoral desk belonging to the current mayor. It's obvious who was backing the museum. Another room illustrates the history of Bayamon complete with the making of *chicharrones* and the daily life of the *jibaro*. There's even a shovel from the 1977 groundbreaking of a Union Carbide emulsions plant. The museum is completed with yet another room of Indian artifacts. From the museum, enter the placid and tranquil Paseo Barbosa. Here, you might see a young girl standing, combing her boyfriend's hair as he sits on a bench. Or a mother sitting with her children, taking a break from shopping. Or pretty schoolgirls with plaid vests and white blouses parading through on their way to and from school. Continue along to the Barbosa Museum (open Mon. to Fri. 8–12, 1–5). The interior of the house contains antique furniture, a small library, and memorabilia relating to Jose Celso Barbosa, journalist, physician, and political head of the pro-statehood Republican Party.

events and festivals: The traditional *fiesta patronales* titled *Fiestas de Cruz* is held in early May. Although this event has its origin in the 18th C., many of the original traditions connected with it have been lost. Once held in a local house, the main event (carrying the cross up the nine steps) now takes place along the Paseo Barbosa. Traditionally, a nine-step altar is prepared and lavishly adorned with flowers and royal palm leaves; candles are placed on each step. After the recitation of *El Rosario Cantao de la Santa Cruz* each night, the cross is moved up one step higher until, on the ninth night, it reaches the top. Traditional refreshments like *guarapo de cana* (sugarcane juice) are served at the end of each night's service. Artisans' festivals are held throughout the year.

shopping and crafts: Local craftspeople sell their wares in Central Park each Sunday. A feminist-run handicraft center, El Centro Feminista, is located at Calle F No. 8 Hnas., Davilas, Bayamon. Ariadina Saez, Calle 6A QQ19, Urbanizacion Cana, carves wooden flower replicas. For information call Bayamon Tourism Office at 780–3056, ext. 280 or 281. Or visit them in their offices on the first floor of the surrealistically modern Alcaldia.

FROM SAN JUAN

San Juan can serve as an excellent base for becoming acquainted with the island, especially if you are renting (or have) your own vehicle; a good portion of the island may be comfortably explored in a day's excursion. Destinations like El Yunque, Loiza Aldea, and Humacao make good daytrips. There are also many small towns like Gurabo, Guaynabo, and Cidra which offer the visitor with limited time an inside look at Puerto Rican life. Aguas Buenas to the S is noted for its caves. Experienced spelunkers may enter them along Carr. 794. Caguas (pop. 173,961) is the largest inland town on the island. **Dorado and beyond:** Reachable either by car, limousine, or small plane, Dorado is the island's oldest resort town. Hyatt Dorado Beach and Hyatt Regency Cerromar Beach are famed for their pools, golf courses, and casinos. A shuttle bus runs between the two resorts on the half hour. Restaurants in the area include: Ladrillo, 224 Mendez Vigo in town; La Terraza, Calle Marginal parallel to Carr. 693; Los Naborias, Call. 690; and La Familia, Carr. 690 on the way to Playa Cerro Gordo. Reserva Forestal de Vega Alta is located past Vega Alta on Carr. 2. Farther on is Manati. Founded in 1738, it has a number of attractive Victorian houses. Here, Hacienda La Esperanza, a 2,265-acre restored sugar plantation was once one of the largest on the island. Transformed into a living historical farm by the Conservation Trust of Puerto Rico, it may be visited with their permission. The entire U.S. supply of Valium and Librium is also produced in this town. Six beaches— Playa Mar Chiquita, Playa Tortuguero, Playa Chivato, Playa de Vega Baja, Playa Cerro Gordo, Playa de Dorado and a freshwater lagoon (Laguna Tortuguero)—lie along a series of winding roads running up the coast to the N. Find them using a

good roadmap. **heading east:** On the eastern outskirts of San Juan are the Club Gallistico cockfighting pit and public beach at Isla Verde and, farther on, the Roberto Clemente Sports City. Dedicated to the memory of the famous Pittsburgh Pirate baseball demigod who died in a 1972 aircrash, *Ciudad Deportiva* has facilities for teaching sports to deprived children. Open daily 9–12, 2–7, it's located on Calle Icurregui off the Los Angeles Marginal Rd. in Carolina. A bit farther near Pinones along Carr. 187 lies Boca de Cangrejos ("Point of the Crabs")—a fishing village with a yacht club and tour boat launch. Sat., Sun., and holidays from noon *La Paseadora* (tel. 791–0755) tours the Torrecilla Lagoon amidst mangrove swamps and the cries of the sanctuary's birds. Heading east of San Juan, near Fajardo and within easy reach of the sideroad to El Yunque is Luquillo, the most famous beach in Puerto Rico. At the end of each day (5PM), a white ambulance with screaming siren runs along the beach. Admission is free, but parking costs $1. Playas San Miquel and Convento stretch on to the E. Stay at Parador Martorell, 6A Ocean Drive (tel. 721–2884, 889–3975).

by *publico:* *Publicos* leave from Old San Juan, Stop 18 in Santurce, and from Rio Piedras. In general, it is easiest to head W towards Arecibo from Bayamon (Old San Juan), or Stop 18, and head S from Rio Piedras or Caguas. To head E from Rio Piedras is easiest. A bus leaves at uncertain intervals from the vicinity of the P.O. in Old San Juan for Barranquitas. *Publicos* for Caguas leave from a stop across from the Teatro Tapia. Hitchers (keeping in mind that Puerto Ricans may be reluctant to pick them up) will do well to take transport out of the urban congestion to a place where a thumb has room to breathe.

internal flights: Eastern and American fly to Mayaguez and Ponce daily. Vieques Air Link flies from San Juan's Isla Grande to Vieques. Flamenco flies to Culebra from Isla Grande.

Luquillo Beach

PUERTO RICO AND
THE VIRGIN ISLANDS

for St. Thomas: Virgin Islands Seaplane Shuttle is both the most pleasurable way to fly and the most convenient. They land on the water, right near the center of town. Aerovirgin, Eastern, TWA, and American also fly. **for St. John:** Once in St. Thomas, take a ferry to St. John from Charlotte Amalie ($5) or Red Hook ($2). Or fly with Virgin Islands Seaplane Shuttle. **for St. Croix:** The same airlines fly. Vieques Air Link flies from Vieques. **for the British Virgin Islands:** Air BVI, Eastern Metro, and American Eagle fly to Tortola daily; Air BVI, Eastern Metro, and American Eagle fly to Virgin Gorda daily.

for the continental United States: Most cities are readily accessible through direct or interconnecting flights. Airlines include BWIA, Delta, American, TWA, and Eastern (see "Getting There" under "Introduction"). If traveling to the airport during rush hour, be sure to allow plenty of time.

NORTHEASTERN PUERTO RICO

LOIZA ALDEA AND ENVIRONS

Named after the Indian princess Luisa who died fighting beside her lover, the Spaniard Mejia, this area is the sole remaining center of Afro-Hispanic culture on the island. The municipo itself is divided into four parts—Pinones, Plaza, Mediana Baja, Mediana Alta. Its history dates back to the 16th C. when African slaves were brought in to work the sugarcane fields and pan for gold in the river. They were supplemented by escaped and recaptured slaves from other islands. Today, the majority of the 40,000 population are freed descendants of these Yoruba slaves. The local leadership is trying to deny the presence of African influence in the area, attempting to substitute Indian instead, because there is no political capital to be gained from being black in Puerto Rico. The town itself was founded in 1719, and its San Patricio Church (begun 1646) is the island's oldest active parish church. Loiza is one of the three poorest municipalities in Puerto Rico.

getting there: Possibly the most exciting part of the trip. Take the A7 bus from Old San Juan's Ochoa bus station to the end of the line in Pinones where many stalls serve traditional, African-influenced foods. From Pinones onward the feel of Africa is in the air. Hitch a ride, continue along the battered, sand-covered asphalt road which runs six miles along unspoiled white sand beaches (nicknamed the "lovers' lane of Puerto Rico"). Then cross the Espiritu Santo River bridge which spans the Rio Grande de Loiza, the island's roughest

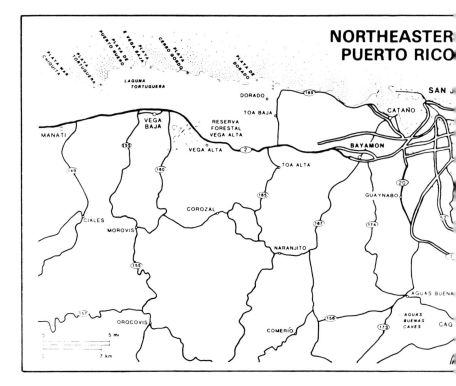

and only navigable river. An alternate but less spectacular route is to take a *publico* from Rio Piedras plaza.

accommodations: Stay at Centro Vacacional U.I.A. (tel. 876–1446).

food: Restaurants include the El Parilla, Carr. 187, km 6.2; and Dona Hilda, Carr. 188, int. 951.

Fiesta Patronales De Loiza

Loiza's three-day tribute to Santiago (St. James) is the most famous fiesta on the island. St. James, first of Christ's disciples to be martyred, made a comeback during the Middle Ages when, descending from the skies on horseback, he slaughtered

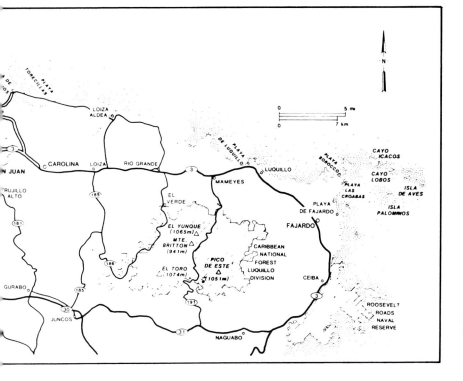

many Moors, thus ensuring a Spanish victory. His popularity with the conquistadore crowd confirmed by this action, he became their patron saint in the Old World as well as the New. Yoruba slaves were forbidden by their Catholic masters to worship the god of their choice, the omnipotent Shango, god of thunder, lightning and war. Noting the resemblance between their god and the Catholic saint, they worshipped Shango disguised as Santiago. In the early part of the 17th C., a fisherman on his way to work found a statuette of a mounted Spanish knight hidden in a cork tree, and he took it home. When he returned to the house, the statue was nowhere in sight. Returning to the tree he again found it secreted, and brought it back home only to have the same thing happen. After the third occurrence, he took the statue to the local priest who, identifying it as Santiago, blessed it. The statue ceased wandering, and the local patron saint festivities commenced. Today, there are three images, the later two brought from 19th C. Spain. Homage is paid to each image on separate days. The original, primitively carved statue, known as *Santiaquito* or "Little James," has been dedicated to children. The others are dedicated to men and women respectively. *Mantenedoras* ("caretakers") take care of each of the three statues; they organize raffles and collect donations. Strings of *promesas* (silver charms) hanging from the base of the statues, are gifts from grateful devotees. These *promesas* are fashioned in the shape of the part of a body to be cured.

the festival: For nine days before the fiesta begins on 26 July, the *mantenedora* of Santiago de los Caballeros holds prayer sessions at her house during which elderly women and children chant rosaries and couplets honoring the saint. On the first day of the festival, a procession led by a flag bearer proceeds to Las Carreras, the spot where the original statue appeared. Stopping at the houses of other *mantenedoras* along the way, the statues are brought out and both carriers and flag bearers kneel three times. The Loiza festival is famous all over Puerto Rico for the beauty and uniqueness of its costumes. *Vejiantes*, who represent devils, wear intricately crafted, colorfully painted coconut masks adorned with horns along the tops and sides. *Locas*, female impersonators with blackened faces, and exaggerated bosoms, and wearing clothes that don't match, pretend to sweep the streets and porches along the way. *Caballeros*, who represent Santiago, wear brightly colored clothes, ribbons and bells, and a soft wire mask painted with the features of a Spanish knight. *Viejos* wear shabby clothes and masks made from shoe boxes or pasteboard. Recently, the festival has been modified; outsiders, who know little of the traditions involved, now make up the majority of the participants. Consequently, the festival has become something of a carnival with salsa music replacing the indigenous *bomba y plena*. The festival is also becoming confused with Halloween: in 1982, E. T. won the prize for best costume.

crafts: Ayala family, Carr. 187, km 6, in Mediana Alta, makes and sells the best festival masks. Before his death in 1980, the family patriarch Castor Ayala was the preeminent mask

NORTHEASTERN PUERTO RICO ACCOMMODATIONS

KEY: S = single, D = double; T = triple; CP = Continental Plan (Breakfast served); pw = per week; B = beach in vicinity; P = pool; C = casino.

NOTE: Rates are given as a guideline only; price fluctuations can and will occur. Summer season generally runs 4/15–11/15 or 12/15; check with hotel concerned for specifics. Hotel addresses are completed with "Puerto Rico." Area code is 809. Accommodation tax of 6% applies to all listings.

ADDRESS	TELE-PHONE	WINTER			SUMMER			# OF ROOMS	NOTES
		S	D	T	S	D	T		
La Ceiba, Carr. 959, Rio Grande	722–3250 887–7000	80	95		65	80		100	B, C
Parador Martorell, 6A Ocean Drive, Luquillo	889–2710 721–2884	35	45–56		25	36–38		7	
FAJARDO									
Delicias, Carr. 195, Puerto Real, Fajardo	863–1818	25	30	50	30	35	50	20	CP
Family Guest House, Carr. 987, Fajardo	863–1193	28–33	37–43	47–54	28–33	37–43	47–54	12	P
VIEQUES									
Banana's Flamboyan, Barrio Esperanza, Vieques	741–8700	48	48		40			7	P
La Casa del Frances, Barrio Esperanza, Vieques	741–3751	69	69		55			19	P
Ocean View, Calle Plinio Peterson, Vieques	741–3966	17–32	32		17–32	32		32	
Sea Gate Guest House, Barriada Fuerte, Vieques	741–4661	40–50	40–50	60	40–50	40–50	60	16	B

(continued)

Northeastern Puerto Rico Accommodations (continued)

ADDRESS	TELE-PHONE	WINTER			SUMMER			# OF ROOMS	NOTES
		S	D	T	S	D	T		
VIEQUES (continued)									
Parador Villa, Esperanza, Vieques	741–8675	48–68	56–76		48–68	56–76		50	B, P
CULEBRA									
Posada La Humaca, 68 Castelar St., Dewey, Culebra	742–3516	20	25		40			6	
Punta Aloe Villas, Punta Aloe, Culebra	742–3167	450 pw			inquire			5	
Villa Boheme, Ensenada Honda, Culebra	742–3508	400 pw			350 pw			5	

maker in Loiza. At Carr. 951, km 7, hm. 3, lives potter Ricardo Rivera.

from Loiza: Return to the plaza to catch a *publico* back to San Juan, or cross the bridge to return via Pinones.

El Yunque and the Caribbean National Forest

Forty km SE of San Juan, the Luquillo Mountains rise abruptly from the coastal plain. Although El Toro (3,526 ft./ 1075m) is actually the highest, the area is called El Yunque after the 3,493 ft. (1065m) peak. The Indian name *yuque* (white land) was transformed by the Spanish into *yunque* (anvil) which the peak does resemble when viewed from the north. Luquillo is a corruption of the supreme being *Yukiyu*, who the Indians believed lived among the mountainous summits. The only tropical forest in the U.S. National Forest sys-

El Yunque

tem, its 27,846 acres contain 75% of the virgin forest remaining in Puerto Rico, the headwaters of eight major rivers, four distinct types of forest, and a wealth of animal and plant life.

getting there: Easily accessible by car, it's less than an hour drive from San Juan. Follow Highway 3 from which Carr. 186

and 191 branch off. While 186 traverses the W boundary of the forest, 191 cuts through its heart. Hiking trails branch off this road. A landslide has closed 191 to traffic at km 13.5 so it's no longer possible to pass through to the south. Hitching along 186 and 191 can be slow, and there's no public transportation through the forest.

history: First protected under the Spanish Crown, the 12,400 acres of Crown Forest were proclaimed the Luquillo Forest Reserve by President Theodore Roosevelt in 1903. Since the creation of the first Forest Service office in the area in 1917, the reserve area has continued to grow; the name was changed to Caribbean National Forest in 1935.

flora: Encouraged by the more than 100 billion gallons of water that fall on the forest each year, the vegetation proliferates. There are four different types of forest which support 250 tree species, more than in any other National Forest. Only six of these 250 can be found in the continental United States. On the lower slopes is the *tabonuco* forest. Nearly 200 species of trees can be found here along with numerous small but attractive orchids. The dominant tree, the *tabonuco*, can be recognized by its whitish bark which peels off in flakes. Growing in valleys and along slopes above 2000 ft. is the *colorado* forest. These short, gnarled trees often have hollow trunks. Many are 1,000 years or more old. In one difficult-to-reach area is a 2,500-year-old *colorado* tree with a circumference of 23 ft., 10 inches. The palm forest, at the next level, is composed almost completely of *sierra* palms complemented by a few *yagrumos*. Masses of ferns and mosses grow underneath as well as on the trees. Limited to the highest peaks and ridges, the dwarf forest, composed of trees 12 ft. high or less, has vegetation (mosses, liverworts) which grow on the ground, tree trunks, and even on leaves.

fauna: Many rare species are found here, including the green, blue, and red Puerto Rican parrot (Amazona uttata), a protected species. Once common throughout the island, less than 50 now survive within the forest confines. Other birds, like the Puerto Rican tanager, the bare-legged owl, the quaildove, and the scaled pigeon, although rare elsewhere, are common here.

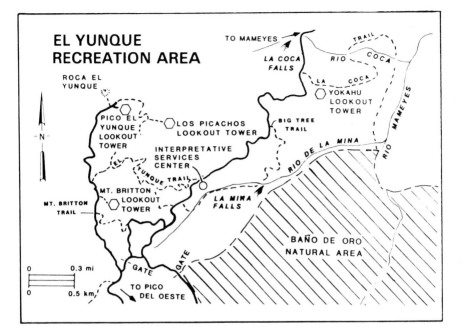

Snakes are scarce, poisonous ones nonexistent; *coqui* frogs croak from every corner, and small fish, shrimp, and crayfish live in the streams.

hiking: Among the 50 km of hiking trails, the principal ones include the El Yunque, Mt. Britton, Big Tree, and El Toro (also called Tradewinds). Trailheads are located on Carr. 186 at km 10.6 and on Carr. 191 at km 13.5. While La Coca Falls and Yohaku Lookout Tower are on or near 191, you must hike to reach La Mina Falls or Pico El Yunque and Los Picachos Lookout Towers. From the top of El Yunque on a clear day it's possible to see St. Thomas or even as far as the British Virgin Islands. Reach El Toro (392 ft., 1074 m), one of the most remote peaks in the area, by the trail of the same name which begins near the aviary and workers' housing area along Rte. 191 at km 13.5. Follow the ridge W to the summit before descending to Cienage Alta, a forest ranger station located along Carr. 186. An alternative is to begin hiking at km 20, five or six km from Florida. Bring food (there's only one restaurant), water-

proof clothing, hiking boots, and a compass. The trails are well maintained, but no fresh drinking water or toilet facilities are available. Although locals drink out of the mountain streams, it's not advisable unless the water has been treated first. Mamayes, along Rte. 3, is the last place to buy food. **note:** The El Yunque area has a bad reputation regarding theft so leave *nothing* of value in your car, and exercise like caution while hiking in the area.

practicalities: Best place to orient yourself is at the Sierra Palm Interpretive Service Center at km 11.6 on Carr. 191 (open 9–5 daily). Obtain additional information by calling the Carolina Field Office (tel. 877–2875, 753–4936), or by writing to Caribbean National Forest, Box B, Palmer, Puerto Rico. Topographical maps are available (for $1) in the field office (open weekdays) at the base of the forest. Buy Puerto Rican snacks at stands along Carr. 191; meals are served at El Yunque Restaurant inside the park at the Service Center. Camping is permitted in most areas of the forest; permits are available at the Service Center. Nearest *parador* is Parador Martorell (tel. 889–2710), 6A Ocean Drive, Luquillo. See chart for details.

Fajardo

A small, sleepy town, it only comes alive during its patron saint festival (Santiago Apostol) every 25 July. It once served to supply pirates, and today it serves as a yachting haven. Offlying cays include Icacos, Palominos, Palominitos, Diablo, and Cayos Lobos. *Publicos* run to the outlying areas of Las Croabas and La Playa-Puerto Real from the plaza. There's nothing much in Las Croabas either except Soroco Beach and a few restaurants. La Playa has a customs house, post office, and ferry terminal.

accommodations: Pitch a tent within the confines of Soroco Beach for $6 per tent. The hotels here are the medium priced

Rainforest, El Yunque

Delicias (tel. 863–1818) and Family Guest House (tel. 863–1193).

from Fajardo: Publicos for Luquillo, Rio Piedras, Juncos, Humacao, etc. leave from the town *plaza*. **for Culebra:** Ferry leaves on Sat., Sun., holidays, at 9 AM; Mon. at 9:15 via Vieques. Cargo ferry departs Tues. to Sat. at 4 ($2.25, it takes two hours). **for Vieques:** Ferry daily at 9:15 and 4:30. Cargo ferry departs Mon. to Fri. at 7 and 11 AM ($2, takes one hour, 30 min.). Vieques Air Link also flies daily. **for Icacos:** Rent a sailboat or sail your own to this deserted island. Camping permitted.

Vieques fishing boats

VIEQUES

Seven miles off the eastern coast of Puerto Rico, this island paradise has a special, distinct magic. Its name comes from the Taino word bieques ("small island"). Horses roam freely all over the island, dotted with the ruins of pineapple and sugar plantations and more than 40 magnificent beaches. Undoubtedly, Vieques would have become one of the major tourist destinations in the Caribbean were it not for the fact that over 70% of its 26,000 acres was confiscated by the U.S. military in 1941. Locals have suffered much at their hands: noise from air and sea target bombardment, annoying in itself, was devastating when coupled with the structural damage to buildings and the dramatic decrease in the fishing catch caused by sea pollution. Population plummeted from 14,000 in 1941 to the present 8,000; Many left to find work in San Juan, St. Croix, or elsewhere. Bombing has now diminished, much of the land has now been let out for grazing purposes, and military maneuvers have been substantially reduced (though Vieques was the site of a rehearsal for the 1983 Grenada invasion). A cultural festival is held in Isabel Segunda every February.

history: First explored in 1524 by Capt. Cristobal de Mandoza, former governor of Puerto Rico, Vieques was occupied at various times by the British and French until it was formally annexed by Puerto Rico in 1854.

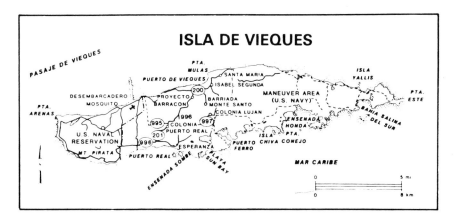

ISLA DE VIEQUES

getting there: A bumpy but beautiful hour-long trip by launch from Fajardo. Pass by Isleta Marina, Palominos, Lobos, Isla de Ramos, and other small islands. Passenger ferries leave daily from La Playa at 9:15 and 4:30. Cargo ferries (which also carry cars and bicycles) leave Mon. to Fri. at 7 and 11. **by air:** Vieques Air Link flies from San Juan's Isla Grande daily, as well as from Fajardo, and St. Croix.

Isabel Segunda

An exceptionally attractive town with many shops selling flowers and a 121-year-old church. Locals ride horses through the main streets while dogs sleep placidly under cars. The town plaza has a bust of Simon Bolivar, who paid a visit to Vieques in 1816, and a 19th C. city hall.

Fort Isabella Segunda: The last Spanish bastion undertaken in the Caribbean (1843), this fort, which dominates the town, was never finished. To get there turn right at the plaza and follow the hill up. It is meticulously restored with beautifully finished wooden staircases, cannon, etc. Inside, a watchman naps to the sound of a blaring radio. **others:** Puntas Mulas Lighthouse is nearby. Davies Base is just outside town. At the entrance obtain permission to visit the beautiful and isolated Green, Red, and Blue beaches, imaginatively named by the Navy. According to legend, a 16th C. island chief hid the sacred treasures of his tribe from the *conquistadores* in a large cave at the top of Mt. Hirata, highest point on the island. The roar you hear inside the cave is his ghost. Archaeological digs are being conducted at La Hueca. Mosquito, the long pier on the isolated NW coast, was built to shelter the British fleet in the event England fell to Germany in WW II. A local conservation group (The Vieques Conservation Trust, Box 1472, Vieques, PR 00765) is endeavoring to preserve Puerto Mosquito, one of the world's last phosphorescent bays.

accommodations: There are many small but not especially cheap hotels in town including Hotels Alvarez, Depakos, Carmen, and Vieques. The Ocean View (tel. 741–3696) is on Plinio Peterson.

food: Small cafeterias abound. The Panaderia, on the main street, has sweets made using local fruits and parcha juice. Also try El Yate, Starboard Light Cafe, Ocean View Restaurant, and Boricua Bar. A very attractive ice cream and frozen banana place is across the street.

Esperanza

Second largest community on the island. Taxis ($1) meet arriving ferries. The 1963 film, *Lord of the Flies,* was filmed here; see the hangar-like structure—now incorporated into the grounds of a government-sponsored parador—that remains. Many eccentric expatriates live in this area. Meet garrulous but personable Irving who runs La Casa Del Frances. Or,

Vieques

rather, he'll meet you. There's a *balneario* at Sunbe (Sun Bay) beach, a long, gorgeous stretch of palm trees and placid ocean. Hike to Navio and Media Luna beaches nearby. The latter has a cave at one end. There's also a dive shop and night excursions to the phosphorescent bay.

accommodations: It's possible to camp at the *balneario* at Sun Bay ($4 per tent). Note, however, that this beach is notorious for thieves—*never* leave anything unattended. Villa Posada Parador has the least expensive accommodation. Other alternatives are Banana's Guest House (Barriada Fuerte, Tel. 741–8700), Sea Gate (Barricada Fuerte, tel. 741–4661), and Irving's La Casa de Frances (Barrio Esperanza, tel. 741–3751)

food: Villa Posada Parador has delicious, authentic, reasonably priced food (like fish *asopao*, $3). Fresh, piping-hot traditional Puerto Rican bread is available early mornings at Gerena Bakery. Colmado Lydia, next door, is well stocked with provisions.

CULEBRA

This miniature archipelago, consisting of the seven-by-four-mile island of Culebra, and 23 other islands, cays, and rocks, is completely unspoiled and set apart from the world. Twenty-two miles E. of Fajardo, much of the land, which includes dry scrub and mangrove swamps, has been designated as a National Wildlife Refuge. The lack of rainfall not only ensures good weather but has the secondary effect of causing low sedimentation—thus producing healthy coral reefs and remarkably clear water.

getting there: Cheapest and best is to take a *publico* from Rio Piedras to the dock at Fajardo. Then board the ferry, which takes a scenic two hours to Dewey on Culebra. A passenger ferry ($2.25) leaves on Sat., Sun., and holidays at 9 and Mon. at 9:15. Cargo ferries leave Tues. to Sat. at 4. The difference between cargo and passenger ferries is chiefly that the passenger ferries leave on time. A ferry also runs from Vieques to

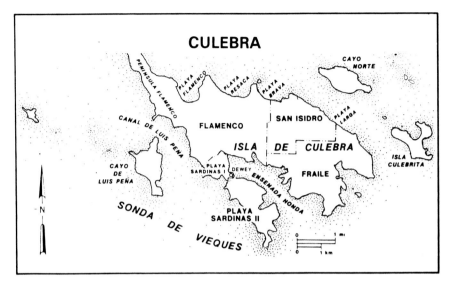

Culebra ($2) on Sat. and Sun. at 11:00, and Mon. at 12:30. An alternative is the 20-min. flight with Flamenco from San Juan's Isla Grande Airport.

history: Under Spanish rule, Culebra and surrounding islands were designated as Crown lands. Transfer to the U.S. in 1898 specified that these lands be used for their "highest and best use." Accordingly, an executive order Roosevelt signed in 1903 surrendered the lands to Navy control. Eight years later, Roosevelt, after reconsidering the matter, ordered that the lands serve the secondary purpose of a "preserve and breeding ground" for native seabirds. In 1936, the Navy (perhaps assuming noise improves fertility among nesting seabirds) began strafing and bombarding Culebra and surrounding islands. Even today, Flamenco Peninsula, a tern nesting area, is dangerous to explore on foot because of unexploded bombs. Despite long years of protest, both by locals *and* by the commonwealth government, bombing still continues. Since 1975, the local population has swelled to more than 2,000.

flora and fauna: The Culebra group has a huge sea bird population; several species have developed large breeding colonies on Flamenco Peninsula and surrounding offshore cays. Of the

Culebra beach

more than 85 species, the most numerous is the sooty tern which arrives to nest between May and October. The sooty tern's eggs are highly prized by local poachers. There are four other species of terns, three of boobies, the laughing gull, Caribbean martin, osprey, and other birds. Brown pelicans, an endangered species, live in the mangrove trees surrounding Puerto de Manglar on Culebra's E side. Small herds of cattle stroll amidst the bombed wrecks of army tanks. The seldom-seen Culebra giant anole (a huge lizard), resides in the forested areas of Mount Resaca. Four species of sea turtles breed on Culebra's beaches: the Atlantic loggerhead and green sea turtles, the hawksbill, and the leatherback. Leatherbacks may reach a length of 6.5 feet (two m) and weigh up to 500 kg. These turtles have been exiled from one Caribbean beach to another by poachers and developers. Here too, despite the threat of stiff penalties under the Endangered Species Act, local poachers value the eggs as a protein source and an aphrodisiac. As part of a well-developed, interdependent ecosystem,

Culebra's flora is inseparable from its fauna. Mangrove forests surrounding the coasts provide a roosting ground for birds above the water while sheltering sea anemones, sponges, and schools of small fish among the tangle of stiltlike roots in the shallow water. Nearly 80% of Culebra's coastline is bordered by young and old coral reefs. Multicolored miniature mountain ranges of brain, finger, elkhorn, and fire corals shelter equally colorful and numerous schools of tropical fish.

crafts: Amparo Rivera Rios, Barriada Clark Casa No. 274, carves coqui frog replicas and makes articles with snail shells. Rosa Garcia de Feliciano, Calle Escudero 63, makes ceramics and articles from snail shells.

from Culebra: Passenger ferries depart Sat., Sun., and holidays at 3 and Mon. (via Vieques) at 1:30. Cargo ferries depart Tues. to Sat. at 7 AM. Flamenco Airways flies daily to San Juan's Isla Grande Airport.

Dewey: When the Navy moved onto Culebra in 1903, locals living in settlements scattered all over the island were forcibly resettled in the newly created town of Dewey (or Puebla), built on what had formerly been a swamp. This small town has five *colmados* (grocery stores) and a couple of hardware stores. No movie theaters or (thankfully) video arcades. Only time the town comes to life is during the fiesta of La Virgen del Carmen on 17 July. Bring your mask and snorkel because the real life is under the water. A pair of binoculars will also come in handy for viewing bird life.

practicalities: A small information service operates inside City Hall. For additional information on the island (including information on temporary rentals) write them at Box 56, Culebra, PR 00645. For information on visiting refuge areas, it's best to write in advance to Refuge Manager, Lower Camp, Fish and Wildlife Service, General Delivery, Culebra, PR 00645. Currently, camping has been prohibited on Flamenco Beach because of the risk of damaging turtle nesting sites. It's possible to camp on Zoni, a totally isolated beach on the island's E side, but you have to be completely provisioned, including water. Hotels include Posada la Hamaca, Calle Castelar 68 (tel.

Culebra

742-3516) and Villa Boheme (Ensenada Honda, tel. 742-3508). Weekly room rates at the latter include use of kitchen, car, boats, and windsurfers (see chart for rates). Restaurants include Maria's Deli, El Pescador, El Batay, and the more de-luxe Club Seabourne. Good snorkeling at Punta Molinas at the NW and at Punta del Soldado to the S.

Culebrita: Can be reached only by fishing boat or private yacht. Its century-old stone lighthouse overlooks a large bay and lagoon. Along with neighboring Luis Pena Cay to the W, it is a wildlife refuge site open to the public for daytime use. Other cays require special use permits available from the Fish and Wildlife Service, Box 510, Boqueron, PR 0622. Heavily covered with vegetation including gumbo-limbo trees, frangipani, and bromeliads, the island provides haven for many rare and endangered species of animals and birds. Red-billed tropic birds live in cliffs along the island's E shore while mangrove swamps are home to birds and marinelife. A 1980 plan, now discarded, would have transferred ownership to the Puerto Rican government so that the island could have been converted to recreational use, a move which would have been ecologically disastrous.

SOUTHEASTERN PUERTO RICO

Roosevelt Roads: Located near the town of Ceiba and Playa Naguabo, this is the most important American base in the Caribbean, home of the Atlantic Fleet Weapons Range, the most advanced technical training area in the entire Atlantic. "Springboard," the full NATO fleet annual exercises, are conducted from here.

Humacao: A small inland town whose fiesta patronales takes place around 8 December. Palmas Botanical Gardens, 130 Candalero Abajo, has 208 acres (84 ha) of plants and trees plus a greenhouse. Playa Humacao is nearby. **accommodations:** Hotel Palace (tel. 850–4180), Ave. Cruz Ortiz Stella is right in town. Cabins are rented out at Centro Vacacional Punta Santiago by Fomento for $20 per night (see "Accommodations" under "Introduction").

Cayo Santiago: A small island off the coast containing a large colony of rhesus monkeys which are being specially bred for scientific experiments by the U.S. Public Health Service. The monkeys were trapped in India in 1938 by C. Ray Carpenter, a pioneer in primate field studies who recognized the need for a "wild" rhesus population in a controlled environment. Victimized at first by tuberculosis, the monkeys almost starved during the war when grant money ceased. In addition to providing a model for behavioral studies, the monkeys have provided clues in the fight against diabetes and arthritis. Over 300 articles have come from research and field studies performed here since 1978 alone. At present there are 20 scientists on the island. Unfortunately, no visitors are permitted.

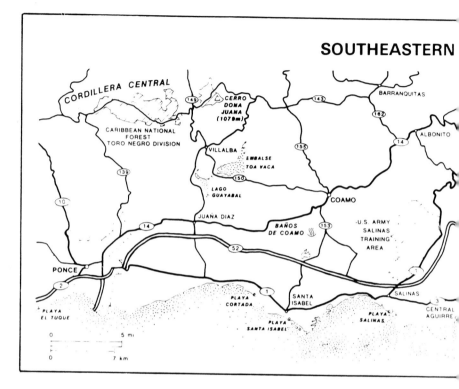

Palmas del Mar: The island's largest resort (located just S of Humacao), and "New American Riviera," the 2,800 acres of this former sugarcane plantation offer golf, riding, beaches, tennis, deep-sea fishing, and, of course, dining and dancing. A great place to escape the island—and everywhere and everything else for that matter. Worth a visit, even if you aren't staying here.

Reserva Forestal Carite (Guavate): This relatively small (6,000 acres) but refreshingly cool (average temperature 72°F) and moist forest reserve contains sierra palms, teaks, and mahogany. It borders Charco Azul, a 30-foot-wide cool blue pool and undeveloped Lago Carite (which features an abandoned housing project). A bit of dwarf forest surrounds the communication tower which mars the 3,000-foot-high Cerro La Santa peak. The reserve also includes Nuesta Madre (a Catholic re-

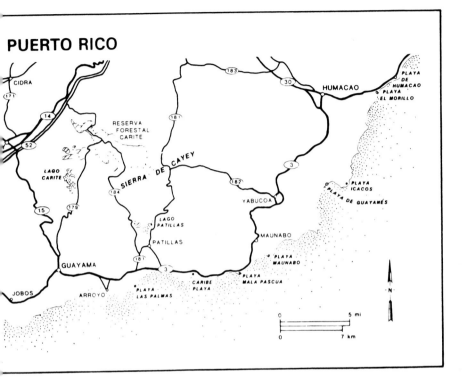

treat), Campamento Guavate (a minimum security penal facility), four picnic areas, and a camping spot. Permission to camp must be obtained in advance from the Department of Natural Resources in Puerto de Tierra, San Juan.

Arroyo: A small town on the W coast founded in 1855. Calle Morse, the main street, was named for the inventor Samuel Morse who arrived in 1848 to oversee installation of telegraph lines. His visit was undoubtedly the most thrilling event that has occurred here before or since the town's foundation. Several 19th-C. houses, with captain's walks on the roofs, were built by New England sea captains who settled here. *Publicos* are the only regular transport. A sugarcane train has been converted to passenger use and is a way of touring the cane fields in the vicinity. It runs from Arroyo to Guayama from 10 AM on Sundays. ($2 adults, $1.50 children). A trolley-on-

SOUTHEASTERN PUERTO RICO ACCOMMODATIONS

KEY: S = single, D = double; T = triple; CP = Continental Plan (Breakfast served); B = beach in vicinity; P = pool; C = casino.

NOTE: Rates are given as a guideline only; price fluctuations can and will occur. Summer season generally runs 4/15–11/15 or 12/15; check with hotel concerned for specifics. Hotel addresses are completed with "Puerto Rico." Area code is 809. Accommodation tax of 6% applies to all listings.

ADDRESS	TELE-PHONE	WINTER			SUMMER			# OF ROOMS	NOTES
		S	D	T	S	D	T		
Palmas del Mar, Carr. 906, Humacao	852–6000	170	190	210	75–110	115–130	125–140	278	CP, B, P, C
Caribe Playa, Carr. 3, km 112, Patillas	863–3339	49			59			36	B
Marina de Salinas, 6–8 Chapin, Salinas	824–3185 752–8484	35			35		B	16	B
Banos de Coamo, Carr. 546, km 1, Coamo	825–2186 721–2884	35	40		48	59		48	B, P
PONCE									
Melia, 2 Calle Cristina, Ponce	842–0260	55–65	60–70		45–65	55–70		80	
Ponce Holiday Inn, Carr. 2, km 221.2, Ponce	844–1200	92–110	107–125		98–145	108–155		120	P

wheels tours the town of Arroyo on Sat. from the port and on Sun. from the train station. The Auberge Olimpico, off the Salinas toll booth on the Ponce Expressway, provides modern training facilities (including pool, track and field course, baseball and soccer fields, and a children's park) for Olympic athletes which visitors may use. Open daily, 8 AM-10 PM, tel. 724–2290. **accommodations:** Cabins (and campsites) at Punta Guilarte are rented out by Fomento to bona fide family groups for $20 per night. There is a two-night minimum stay, and they must be booked 120 days in advance. For more information see "Accommodations" under "Introduction."

Aibonito: Aibonito (from Artibonicu, "River of the Night," the Taino name for this region), a small but colorful town set in a valley and surrounded by mountains, has a Mennonite community, well-tended flower gardens, and boasts Puerto Rico's lowest recorded temperature (40°F in 1911). Once an important tobacco and coffee growing area, Aibonito is now known for its poultry farms and processing plants as well as its factories which produce pharmaceuticals, clothing, electronic goods, and hospital equipment. The town's best known celebration is its Flower Festival. Taking place from the end of June through the beginning of July, colorful flowers (including gardenias, anthuriums, and begonias), gardens, and exhibits occupy 10 acres. **sights:** Standing next to the town plaza, the twin-towered San Jose Church dates from 1825; it was reconstructed in 1978. Now notable only for its spectacular view, Las Trincheras ("the trenches") marks the spot where the last battle of the short-lived American 1898 invasion was fought—a skirmish which took place the day after the armistice had been signed! Another famous panoramic landmark is La Piedra Degetau, a large boulder overlooking the town and on the site of the farm of Federico Degetau Gonzales, former Resident Commissioner in Washington, D.C.

Barranquitas: At 1,800 ft., Barranquitas is not only one of the highest towns on the island, but also one of the most beautifully situated. Viewed from the massive volcanic rocks that cradle it, it resembles a Spanish medieval print. The Catholic church towers above houses which seem to have been built right on top of each other. Its chief claim to fame is as the birthplace of Puerto Rican statesman Luis Munoz Rivera (see "History" under "Introduction"). At the Museo Biblioteca, in the wooden house where he was born in 1859, a small museum displays letters, pictures, newspaper clippings, a car used in his 1915 funeral procession, furniture and other items. Mauseleo de Don Luis Munoz Rivera, Calle Munoz Rivera, located next to the tomb where Don Luis and his son Luis Munoz are buried, documents his funeral vividly with objects and papers relevant to his demise. Also present are the skeleton of a 12-year-old Taino lad and religious relics. Barranquitas celebrates its fiesta patronales, San Antonio de Padua, around 13 June. The National Crafts Fair is held here in July.

vicinity of Barranquitas: Indian relics have been found in a number of caves near the town. Nearly inaccessible, the deep gorge of San Cristobal Canyon located along the road to Aibonito is the most spectacular on the island. Precipitious cliffs, densely covered with vegetation, plunge 500 ft. to a rocky valley where the Usabon River races over boulders, dropping 100 ft. at one point. Catch a glimpse from Rtes. 725 (and side road 7715), 156, and 162. Best of these is from the San Cristobal Development on Rte. 156, km 17.7. An unmarked trail leads into the gorge from here.

Coamo

This small town has its old church set in a plaza enlivened by flowering bouganvillea. Once the site of two flourishing Taino Indian villages, only a solitary Indian remained at the time of the town's founding in 1579. As the third oldest town on the island (after San Juan and San German), its name, San Blas de Illecas de Coamo, was derived from the patron saint of a major landowner—an expatriate from Ilecas, Spain.

sights: The Catholic church is decorated with paintings by internationally renowned Puerto Rican artists Jose Campeche and Francisco Oller. The latter's "Cuadro de las Animas" features a blonde (rumored to be Oller's girlfriend) being tortured in purgatory. One of the church's three bells—said to have sounded so loudly that its vibrations killed fish off the coast and shattered lamps and glass in nearby homes—has been silenced by public pressure for over a century. An elegant two-storey masonry mansion, built by Clotilde Santiago, the town's wealthiest and most powerful farmer and entrepreneur during Spanish rule, still stands at one corner of the plaza. Converted to a museum, it now houses historical memorabilia, gold-plated bathroom fixtures, and mahogany furniture. Call

City Hall (tel. 825–1150) to make an appointment to see the museum. The town's major landmark, however, is not a building but a group of hotsprings. First used by the Indians, the springs gained an international reputation by the end of the 19th century. Some assert that they are the Fountain of Youth Ponce de Leon had heard about from the Indians before taking off to search for it in Florida. To reach them, take the road outside of town going toward the Banos de Coamo Parador, a government-run inn recently built on the site of the Coamo Springs Hotel, which once sheltered the likes of Franklin Delano Roosevelt. Proceeding past the *parador*, turn L to find the springs.

where to stay: Only choice is Banos de Coamo, outside town on Rte. 46, km.

PONCE

Set between the blue of the Caribbean and the green of the Cordillera Central mountain range, Ponce is a city of many names. It is known as La Perla del Sur (The Pearl of the South), la Ciudad Senorial (Manorial City), and La Ciudad de las Quenepas (City of the Honeyberries). Ponce has played host to many prominent islanders, including opera tenor Antonio Paoli, composer Juan Morel-Campos, and painter Miguel Pou. Though it's the second largest city in Puerto Rico (pop. 200,000), Ponce has much more the feeling of a small town than bustling metropolitan San Juan. From the impressive art museum to the colorful firehouse on its main plaza, the city has much to offer the visitor. Established in 1692, Ponce was named after Juan Ponce de Leon y Loaiza, the great-grandson of Puerto Rico's first governor, Ponce de Leon. Originally, Ponce was a town with only two entrances: one would enter either via a mountain road passing by the Church of la Guadalupe or along the road that borders the S coast. Point of entrance was la Ceiba de Cuatro Calles (Ceiba of the Four Streets) which led, as it still does today, to the main streets of Commercio, Cruz, Salud, and Mayor. During 1877–78 when it

Ponce

was granted the title of Ciudad (city), Ponce was already the social, military, and commercial center of the S coast. Its *fiesta patronales* takes place in Feb. when locals don spiked masks made from gourds.

getting there: Approachable by bus from Utuado ($2) or Adjuntas, or by *publico* from Rio Piedras, Santurce, Mayaguez, or other neighboring towns. Eastern and American fly from San Juan's Munoz Marin International Airport.

Sights

Ponce's beautiful plaza with its fountains and gardens is dominated by the sugar-white Cathedral of Our Lady of Guadalupe. Built in 1670, it was destroyed several times by earthquakes. In the center of Plaza Las Delicias, a bronze Luis Munoz Marin, first elected governor of Puerto Rico, gazes out over the

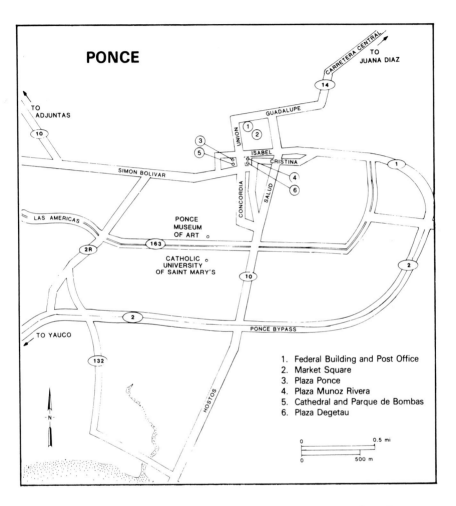

PONCE

TO
JUANA DIAZ

CARRETERA CENTRAL

14

TO
ADJUNTAS

10

GUADALUPE

UNION

1
2

3

5

ISABEL

CRISTINA

4

6

SIMON BOLIVAR

CONCORDIA

SALUD

1

LAS AMERICAS

PONCE
MUSEUM
OF ART

2R

163

CATHOLIC
UNIVERSITY
OF SAINT MARY'S

10

2

2

2

PONCE BYPASS

TO YAUCO

132

HOSTOS

- N -

1. Federal Building and Post Office
2. Market Square
3. Plaza Ponce
4. Plaza Munoz Rivera
5. Cathedral and Parque de Bombas
6. Plaza Degetau

0   0.5 mi

0   500 m

banks, travel agencies, and solitary video game parlor that surround the plaza. Also in the center of the plaza is the Fountain of the Lions, a monument dedicated to eight brave citizens who risked their lives in 1899 to extinguish a fire in the munitions depot that might have spelled disaster for the city, and a monument to Juan Morel Campos, known as the father of the Puerto Rican *danza* (see Music and Dance under Introduction). Born in Ponce in 1857, his *danzas* are still played in Puerto Rico and many of his symphonic works received international recognition. Situated just off the plaza is Ponce's gaudy landmark the *Parque de Bombas* or firehouse. Painted red, green, black, and yellow, it has become the symbol of the city. Sole survivor of several buildings constructed for an agricultural fair held in 1882, it was donated to the homeless firemen in 1885 and has been in active use ever since. Enter and see the second-floor exhibits. From one of the balconies, the

Parque de Bombas, Ponce

municipal band entertains on Sun. nights. Across from the cathedral stands Ponce's newest sight: Casa-Armstrong Proventud, a restored mansion housing a small museum. Open Tues. to Fri., 9–12, 1–4, Sat., Sun., and holidays.

Ponce Museum of Art: Ponce's most renowned attraction is the Ponce Museum of Art on Ave. Las Americas across from Universidad Catolica Santa Maria. Open weekdays 10–12 and 1–5, Sat. 10–4, Sun. 10–5, closed Tuesday, $1.50 admission. Designed by architect Edward Durrell Stone and financed by conservative multimillionaire industrialist and former Governor Don Luis Ferre, this block-long building uses natural light to lend a spacious effect to its hexagonal galleries. It contains the best collection of European art in the entire Caribbean. From an original 400 works, the collection has grown to include more than 1,000 paintings and 400 sculptures. Three sculpture gardens branch off the main floor, and two dynamic, 18th C. polychromed wooden statues carved in Toledo, Spain, representing Europe and America greet the visitor near the entrance. Besides portraits and the representative works of Puerto Rican master painters like Jose Campeche and Francisco Oller, the first floor also contains a 15th C. Siamese Bodhisattva bust, intricate Incan pottery, and fine handblown decorated glass pieces. The second floor holds many fine sculptures and old European thematic religious paintings: plenty of blood, breasts, and skulls. See St. Francis at prayer and Pero feeding Cimon with her breast. Also works by masters like Van Dyck, Reubens, Velazquez, and Gainsborough are included. When visiting the museum weekdays, allow for the fact that it closes one hour for lunch and everyone must leave the building.

others: La Ceiba de Ponce, an enormous 300-year-old silk cotton tree, overhangs Calle Comercio about one km E of the plaza. Once a meeting place for the Taino Indians, it was recreated in one of Franciso Oller's paintings. El Vigia Hill, on Rte.1 near Calle Bertoly, is a famous lookout point surrounded by homes of the wealthy upper class. In the distant past, a watchman, noting the arrival of a visiting merchant vessel, would raise a flag which indicated its nationality. On a clear day, it's possible to see Caja de Muertos offshore, a small island named for its coffin-like shape. Its name may be apt because it includes four endangered plant species (extinct on the mainland) and several endangered lizards as well. Ferries run out to it (Sat. and Sun., $5.50). Its nearby neighbors are Cayo Morillito and Cayo Berberia.

Tibes Indian Ceremonial Center: Located in a suburb of Ponce. Take a *publico* from the vicinity of the *mercado* to get there (open Tues. to Sun. 9–4:30; admission $1.00). Predating the Caguana site near Utuado, it was discovered by Luiz Hernandez, a local resident, in 1974. Archaeological evidence suggests two distinct periods of occupation: during the latter phase of the Igneri culture from A.D. 400–600, and within the pre-Taino period from A.D. 600–1100. Both cultures were similar in terms of diet and lifestyle; cultural differences were due to an influx of new blood from outside or transitions in style over time. The older Igneri period is characterized by animal-shaped amulets, ceramic vessels, and axes. The majority of the 182 graves excavated here, which contained the remains of

Tibes Ceremonial Park

children along with ceremonial offerings, date from this period. Other ceramics, and objects such as frog-shaped amulets, *cemi* figures, and adzes, are from the later pre-Taino period. **bateyes:** Ten ceremonial *bateyes* have been reconstructed. Petroglyphs, with animal and human faces, have been chiseled on some of the stones which delineate the bateyes. The largest *bateye*, measuring 111 by 118 ft., is bordered with walkways containing riverbed stones. The area of Tibes derives its name from these stones; tibes is the Taino word for smooth, riverbed stones. These *bateyes*, known colloquially as ballparks, were multipurpose in use. While some were used for a game resembling soccer, others were used for *areytos*, ceremonial dances in which Indians, drinking beer made from fermented cassava and inhaling hallucinogenic cajoba seeds through a two-pronged pipe, would commune with the gods. There are no records as to what they talked about, but presumably they touched on politics, food, and sex. One elliptical *bateye* is surrounded by triangles, which suggests that it represents the sun. The major archaeological find at Tibes, an adult male skeleton discovered within the foundations of a walkway bordering one of the *bateyes*, has been dated at A.D. 790, which pushes back the date of the earliest known Indian stone constructions by 400 years. Besides the *bateyes*, a small Taino village nearby has been faithfully recreated. There is also a small museum, and bilingual guides are available.

Hacienda Buena Vista: Recently restored by the Conservation Trust, this coffee plantation contains slave quarters, an estate house, and agricultural machinery. Located on Carr. 10, Km 16.8, it's open to groups Wed. and Thurs.; general admission ($4 adults, $1 children) is on Fri. and Sat. with reservations required (tel. 722–5882).

Practicalities

accommodations: Many inexpensive hotels are clustered around the main square. Hotel Comercio is on Calle Comercio. Professional Hotel is at 64 Calle Concordia (tel. 840–0201).

San Jose is at 45 Calle Cristina (tel. 342–0281). Hotel Copamarina Beach Resort is at Carr. 14, Km 5.3 (tel. 724–2735). Hotel Melia is at 2 Cristina (tel. 842–0260, 842–0261). And the Ponce Holiday Inn is at Carr. 2, Km 221.2 (tel. 844–1200).

food: Streets are literally packed with *cafeterias* and restaurants. Fast-food places are strewn along Ave. Las Americas. Established bistros include Rene & Joe's, 3 Las Americas; Anca, 9 Hostos; Aeropuerto at Mercedita Airport; and the restaurants inside the Hotel Melia and Holiday Inn.

entertainment: Ponce's discos include La Nueva Discoteca, Calle Aurora, and Cowboy, Calle Commercio. Latin music can be found at El Sol Restaurant, Ave. Munoz Rivera, in front of Santa Maria Shopping Center. For movies, try the Rivoli on Calle Leon, Ponce Twins, Calle Constacia, and El Emperador at the bypass.

events: The annual patron saint festival of Nuesta Senora de Guadelupe, held from 6–16 Dec., centers on the main plaza. Salsa, merengue, and jazz bands play, and *bomba y plena* dancing is supplemented by *aguinaldo* music. A variety of foods are served, and *artesanias* sell their wares. *Feria Regional de Artesanias*, a crafts fair, is held each Feb., and the *Festival de Bomba del San Anton* is held in November.

crafts and shopping: Antonio Rodriguez Acosta, Calle Martin Corchado 33, makes *torneros* (mortar and pestles). Santerio Domingo Orta works at Calle Lorencita Ferre, Final 139, Sector El Tugue. Juan Alindato, Puerto Viejo No. 18, Playa de Ponce, makes *caretas* (masks). Onofre Rivera Torres, Callejon Nueva Atenas 10, manufactures maracas. Ponce's modern *mercado* is an air-conditioned showplace with fruit and vegetables, spices, bottles of pure honey, gigantic avocados, and drinking coconuts (65¢). Shop 138 has pigs' tails, ears, and snouts for $1 a pound—a great buy! Feet are even cheaper at 55¢ a pound; best quality assured. There's also Nirvana Laundry which undoubtedly offers heavenly service. Botanicas (shops selling spiritualist literature and goods), tailors, and

Ponce carnival masks

other shops are upstairs. At No. 49, charming handmade stuffed cloth black *madama* dolls start at $6.

services: Ponce Tourism Office (tel. 844–5575), located inside recently restored Casa Armstrong-Proventud, Plaza las Delicias (in front of the cathedral), is open Mon. to Fri. 8–12, 1–4:30. At the small municipal library nearby, shorts are verboten under pain of expulsion by the resident police guard.

from Ponce: Numerous *publicos* and very occasional buses depart from the areas surrounding the plaza and mercado for local destinations and Guayama, Yauco, Coamo, etc. Get an early start or you'll feel like a roast chicken while waiting for them to fill up. Linea Atlas Trans Island (tel. 842–1065/4375), with offices on the plaza, will take you to Rio Piedras ($6), Santurce ($8), and directly to Isla Verde Airport ($15). The first of nine *publicos* daily departs at 4AM. Either reserve a seat or just hunt one up when you're ready to leave. **by air:** Eastern and American fly daily to Luis Munoz Marin International Airport from Mercedita Airport.

SOUTHWESTERN PUERTO RICO

YAUCO

Built on a hillside W of Ponce, this small town still has step streets, old houses, great coffee, and a distinctly Spanish-American atmosphere. The Coffee Festival is held here in Feb., while the festival of patron saint Nuestra Senora del Rosario happens around 7 October.

history: Originally known to the Indians as *Coayuco*, the surrounding area was settled by the Spanish, becoming an independent municipality in 1756. Haitian French, Corsicans, and other immigrants began arriving in the early 1800s. Sugarcane and cotton gave way to coffee cultivation. Low in caffeine but rich in taste, Yauco's coffee became famous in Europe for its exceptional quality, soon commanding a high market price. The loss of European markets after the Spanish-American War, combined with the devastation caused by a hurricane in 1899 and competition from mass-producing countries like Brazil and Columbia, sadly led to the decay of the local coffee industry.

practicalities: Only available accommodation is at the modest and inexpensive La Casa Roig, 10 Calle Betances, and at Richard's Hotel, Calle 25 July. *Publicos* go to Ponce ($1.50), Guanica-Guayanilla, and Sabana Grande.

Guanica: Reserva Forestal Guanica, several beautiful beaches, and the place where the Americans landed during the 1898 invasion are all situated around this pleasant town of

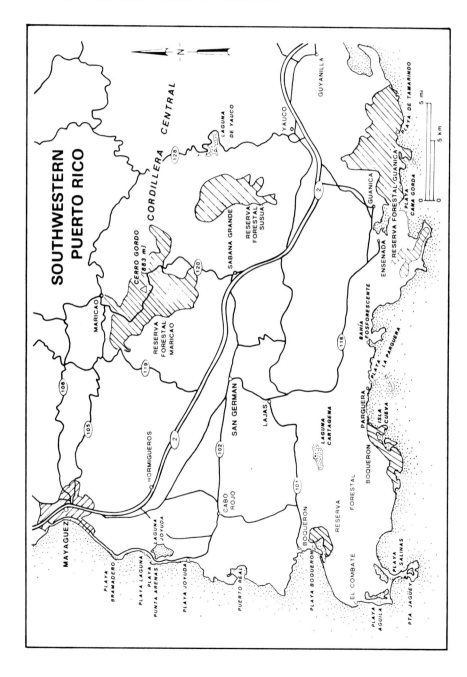

9,000. The reserve itself is one of the finest examples of cactus-scrub-subtropical dry forest in the world. It has recently been designated by the United Nations as a Man and the Biosphere Reserve. Vegetation inside the reserve includes *aroma* (acacia) and *guayacan* (lignum vitae) trees as well as 700 species of plants. The *guabario* (Puerto Rican whippoorwill) survives on the island only in this reserve. Be sure to catch the view of Guanica and the bay from the top of the stone tower. **accommodations:** Copamarina (tel. 842–8300) along Carr. 333, charges $34s, $42d.

Sabana Grande: Founded mostly by Spanish nobility and members of venerable Spanish families. The locals here set up their own government during the Spanish-American War. It lasted days. The *fiesta patronales* of San Isidoro Labrador takes place around 15 May. This small community is chiefly noted for the miracle which occurred here. One day in 1953, a group of schoolchildren chanced upon the Virgin Mary while pausing at a brook near the town. She was wearing a blue robe, white tunic, a neck brooch, and a sash, and sandals. After chatting a few minutes with the children, the Virgin promised to return on 25 May. When a group of 130,000 devotees arrived on that date at the spot, the Divine Lady failed to show up. However, many of the chronic ailments and diseases of those present were reportedly cured on the spot. Many eyewitness reports attest to serious diseases cured by the healing power of the brook where the Virgin was seen. Numerous small shrines and a large chapel have been erected to commemorate the miracles that took place here, and the anniversary of the sighting is commemorated by a Mass yearly. In 1988, an estimated 100,000–400,000 attended and calls continued for official recognition of the sighting by the Catholic Church.

San German

Second oldest and certainly the most attractive town on the island, San German retains its quiet colonial charm and dis-

tinguished architecture. The atmosphere is distinctly Mediterranean. Local legend insists that the swallows of Capistrano
winter here. The town is named after King Ferdinand of
Spain's second wife, Germaine de Foix, whom he married in
1503. Today's population are descendants of the pirates, Corsicans, smugglers, poets, priests, and politicians of days past.
Although the pirates and sugar plantations may be gone for-
ever, a feeling from that era still lingers in the town.

sights: Two rectangular plazas in the center of town face each
other, separated only by the city hall, a former prison. Martin
Quinones Plaza boasts San German de Auxerre Church. Built
in the 19th C., its wooden vault, painted in blue and grey,
simulates a coffered ceiling. The second plaza, Parque de Santo
Domingo, now bordered with black iron and wooden park
benches, was originally a marketplace. The Church of Porta
Coeli ("Gate of Heaven"), the town's main attraction, rises
dramatically from the end of the plaza (open Tues. to Sun. 9–
12, 1–4:30). Twenty-four brick steps lead up to the white walls
of the entrance. Originally constructed by Dominican friars in
1606, it is believed to have been connected by tunnels to the
main monastery which no longer exists. Restoration was completed in 1982. While the palm wood ceiling and tough, brown
ausobo beams are original, the balcony is a reconstruction. It's
set up to resemble a working chapel rather than a museum,
and Mass is held here now only three times a year. Treasures
gathered from all over have been placed along its sides. Exhibits range from choral books from Santo Domingo to a surly
17th C. portrait of St. Nicholas de Bari, the French Santa
Claus. Others include a primitive carving of Jesus found in
San Juan, several lovely 19th C. Senora de la Monserrate
Black Madonna and Child statues, and a representation of
San Cristobal with a part from one of his bones inserted.

near Porta Coeli: The residence of Mrs. Delia Lopez de
Acosta contains decorative murals on the inside. The Perichi
home on Calle Luna is another classic. Mrs. Olivia Perez's
home on Calle Esperanza fulfills the fantasies associated with
having a home in the tropics. The lovely grounds of Inter
American University are on the edge of town just off the road
to Cabo Rojo.

Porta Coeli, San German

accommodations: Parador Oasis is a classically styled hotel on Calle Luna. La Pension is a guesthouse located on the grounds of Inter American University. Rooms come equipped with private bath, two twin beds, sofa bed, and desk. Kitchen and laundry facilities and gym and recreation room are available for use. Prices are $25s, $35d, $40t, $45 quad. For information or booking contact Box 5100, Inter American

SOUTHWESTERN PUERTO RICO ACCOMMODATIONS

KEY: S = single, D = double; T = triple; CP = Continental Plan (Breakfast served); B = beach in vicinity; P = pool; C = casino.

NOTE: Rates are given as a guideline only; price fluctuations can and will occur. Summer season generally runs 4/15–11/15 or 12/15; check with hotel concerned for specifics. Hotel addresses are completed with "Puerto Rico." Area code is 809. Accommodation tax of 6% applies to all listings.

ADDRESS	TELE-PHONE	WINTER			SUMMER			# OF ROOMS	NOTES
		S	D	T	S	D	T		
Copamarina, Carr. 333, Guanica	842–8300 724–2735	42	53		36	46		72	P
SAN GERMAN									
Parador Oasis, Calle Luna, San German	892–1175	45–48	52–54		45–48	52–54		50	P
University Guest House, 206-A del Toro Hall, San German	892–1095 ext. 315, 387	25	35	40	25	35	40		
CABO ROJO									
Parador Boquemar, Carr. 101, Cabo Rojo	851–2158	48			48		41	P	
El Combate Guest House, Carr. 101, 1st St., Parcelas, El Combate, Cabo Rojo	754–9061 851–0001	35			35			17	B
Cuestamar, Carr. 307, km 7.4, Cabo Rojo	851–281845	45		50	45		50	20	P
Parador Perichi's Beach Colony, Carr. 102, km 14.2, Barrio Joyuda, Cabo Rojo	851–3131	41	46		41	46		15	B
LAJAS									
Posada Porlamar, Carr. 304, Lajas	899–4015	35	45	50	35	45	50	18	P

(continued)

Southwestern Puerto Rico Accommodations (*continued*)

ADDRESS	TELE-PHONE	WINTER			SUMMER			# OF ROOMS	NOTES
		S	D	T	S	D	T		
LAJAS (*continued*)									
Viento y Vela Guest House, Carr. 304, km 3.2, Lajas	899–4698	30–35	45	50	30–35	45	50	8	B
Villa Parguera, Carr. 304, Lajas	899–3975	32–55			56			50	B, P
MAYAGUEZ									
Parador El Sol, 9 S.R. Palmer Estate, Mayaguez	834–0303	31–36	39–45		31–36	39–45		40	P
Mayaguez Hilton, Car. 2, km 152.5, Mayaguez	834–7575 724–0161	114–137	137–164		119–145	139–165		145	B, P
La Palma, Calle Menzez Vigo, Mayaguez	834–3800	28–37	36–45		28–37	36–45		47	CP, B
MARICAO									
Parador Hacienda Juanita, Carr. 105, km 23.5, Maricao	838–2550	35	40		35	40		21	P

University, San German, Puerto Rico 00753 (tel. 892–1095, exts. 315, 387).

Hormigueros: This town owes its name, which means "ant hill", to the unique topography of the region. Originally a barrio of San German, later of Mayaguez, it became a distinct town in 1874. Hormigueros is home to the Shrine of Our Lady of Monserrate, a majestic yellow church which towers above the town. According to a 17th C. legend, a peasant working in the field where the church now stands saw an enraged bull charging toward him. After pleading with Our Lady of Monserrate to protect him, he saw the bull stumble and fall; the man managed to escape and the church was erected in thanksgiving. In commemoration of the miracle, the devout arrive on a religious pilgrimage, and each 8 Sept. climb the long bank of steps leading to the church on their hands and knees. See the oil painting by Jose Campeche, which portrays the miracle, on a wall inside the church.

Cabo Rojo: A small town and convenient jumping-off point for Mayaguez or destinations to the south. Founded in 1772, the San Miguel Arcangel Church was erected in 1783 next to the plaza. It reached its peak of prosperity in the 1800s, when immigrants from Spain and other Mediterranean countries, fleeing revolutions in Europe, arrived to take up sugercane cultivation. Today, the canefields have been displaced by pasture for cattle. Cabo Rojo's *fiesta patronales* takes place around 29 September. Joyuda Beach, with its 18 seafood restaurants, is off Carr. 102 to the NW. To the W. nearly half the island's fish are caught at Puerto Real. When it served as Cabo Rojo's port (1760–1860), merchandise and slaves from St. Thomas and Curacao were off-loaded here. At Ostiones, a point of land protruding to the N of Puerto Real, is an important Indian archaeological site. Of special interest to birdwatchers, Laguna Joyuda is 7.5 km NW of town. Its 300 acres (150ha) contains a vast variety of birds including pelicans, martins, and herons. It is luminescent on moonless nights. Beachgoers will want to check out Playa Buye to the SW on Carr. 307. **accommodations:** There are two inexpensive alternatives right in town. Cabo Rojo Guest House, 25 Munoz Rivera, has fine, very clean rooms. Frank Moralles' house at 46 Carmelor resembles a yellow castle. For other accommodations in the area, see Boqueron, La Parguera, and the accommodations chart.

Lajas: Named after the slate found in its vicinity, this small town dates from the early 19th C. Originally a part of San German, it became an independent municipality in 1883. Its *fiesta patronales* (in honor of patron saint Nuestra Senora de la Candelaria) takes place in the beginning of February, which is also the start of the *zatra* or pineapple season for which the area is famous. Great view from the top of Las Animas mountain to the W. A kite festival is held here in mid-March.

Boqueron

Located S of Cabo Rojo and W of San German is the small town of Boqueron, and the western branch of the Bosque Estatal de Boqueron (Boqueron Forest Reserve). Herons perch on mangroves in the bird sanctuary here. The town itself is well known for its extremely beautiful *balneario* (public beach), as well as its oysters and other types of seafood. Its harbor once sheltered pirates like the famous Roberto Cofresi. Cabo Rojo Lighthouse is on Carr. 303. It stands along a spit of land between Bahia Salinas and Bahia Sucia. Beneath the lighthouse, jagged limestone cliffs at Jaguey Point drop 2,000 ft. into the sea. Once inhabited by the lighthouse keepers and their families who occupied the two wings at its base, it is now electrified and automatic. This lighthouse was built in 1881 under Spanish rule in response to pressure from local planters. Behind it lies the Sierra Betmeja, low hills which date back 130 million years. The Salinas salt beds are nearby; salt harvested here is sent off to the Starkist plant in Mayaguez. El Combate, a fishing village to the N at Guaniquilla are Buye and La Mela beaches; the neighboring lagoon at Guaniquilla Point harbors strangely shaped boulders which protrude from and dominate the still waters of the sometimes dry lagoon. Birds squeal and cry overhead. Pirate Roberto Cofresi, who terrorized the coast during the early 19th C., hid out in a cave nearby.

accommodations: The government agency Fomento rents out cabins to "bona fide family groups" (i.e., parents and children) for $20 per night. There is a two-night minimum stay, and they must be booked 120 days in advance. For more information see "Accommodations" under "Introduction." Also in the area: Parado Boquemar, Carr. 101 (tel. 851–2158); Guest House El Combate, Carr. 101, Street 1 (tel. 851–0001, 754–9061); Hotel Cuestamar, Carr. 307, km 14.2; and Parador Perichi's, Carr. 102, km 14.2 (tel. 851–3131). Camping is available around the Cabo Rojo area: Villa Plaza at Denigno Obejo Plaza is on Carr. 301 at km 6.9 (tel. 851–1340). Villa La Mela is at Carr. 307, km 35, Cabo Rojo (tel. 851–1391/2067). Moja-

cascade Camp is at Carr. 301, km 10.1, Playa Combate, Cabo Rojo (tel. 745–0305).

La Parguera

Located off Carr. 304 is the eastern branch of Bosque Estatal De Boqueron, commonly referred to as La Parguera, after the town of the same name. The name itself derives from *pargos*, a type of snapper. This area contains what is probably the most famous marine attraction in Puerto Rico. *La Bahia Fosforescente* (Phosphorescent Bay) contains millions of luminescent dinoflagellates, a microscopic plankton. Any disruption or disturbance causes them to light up the surrounding water. Pick a moonless night and take one of the twice-nightly boats (times vary) departing from Villa Parguera's pier. Dip a hand in the water and watch as sparks of liquid silver run through it. Bahia Mondo Jose, nearby, also has a large population of dinoflagellates. The small town lights up on weekends when there's live entertainment. Offshore are more than 30 mangrove cays. Check on transport out to Mata de la Cay, two miles offshore. Visible from the outskirts of town is Isla Cueva. It's commonly known as Monkey Island because 400 monkeys reside there. Originally from India, they are allowed to pursue their favorite pastimes freely among the trees. Occasionally, a group of scientists arrives to check up on their habits. Rosada Beach is E of town.

accommodations: Posada Porlamar, Carr. 304 (tel. 899–4015); Guest House Viento y Viela, Carr. 304, km. 3.2 (tel 899–4698, 899–3030); Parador Villa Parguera, Carr. 304 (tel. 721–2884, 899–3975).

MAYAGUEZ AND VICINITY

Despite its reputation as a center of industry, this western port, the third largest city on the island, still retains much of the grace and charm suggested by its lovely name, taken from *majagua*—the Indian name for a tree plentiful in the vicinity. In addition to its zoo and agricultural research station, Mayaguez is a good place to base yourself for day trips to Maricao, San German, and the many beaches and small towns in the area.

getting there: Easily approached by publico from San German, Ponce, San Juan, Arecibo, Aguadilla, or Rincon. Eastern and American also fly daily from San Juan's Munoz Marin International Airport.

sights: The city was almost completely destroyed by an earthquake in 1917 and has been largely rebuilt. One of the premier sights is the impressive Plaza de Colon, with its monstrous statue of Columbus, surrounded incongruously by

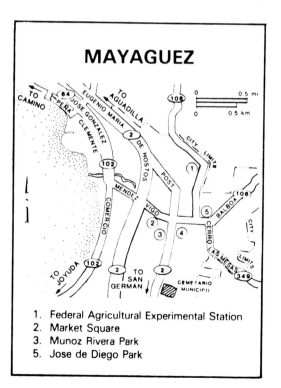

MAYAGUEZ

1. Federal Agricultural Experimental Station
2. Market Square
3. Munoz Rivera Park
5. Jose de Diego Park

statues of Greek maidens. The old post office building is on Calle McKinley nearby, as is the Yaguez Theater. In 1977 this theater was purchased by the federal government and declared a Historical Monument. Renovated, expanded, and modernized at a cost of $4.5 million, it presents all types of stage productions and is a center for artistic, cultural, and educational activities in the community. The Mayaguez Zoo is home of innumerable reptiles, birds, and mammals, presented both in cages and in simulated natural habitats. See everything from Bengal tigers to capybara (world's largest rodents). Located on Carr. 108 at Barrio Miradero; open Tues. to Sun. 9–4:30, $1 admission; tel. 834–8110. Much closer to town is the tropical Agricultural Research Station on Carr. 65, between Calle Post and Carr. 108, located next to the University of Puerto Rico at Mayaguez. Open Mon. to Fri. 7:30–4:30; free admission; tel. 832–2435. Established at the beginning of this century on the site of a former plantation, the grounds present a dazzling array of exotic vegetation ranging from a Sri Lankan cinnamon tree to pink torch ginger to the traveler's tree. While you're here be sure to check out the Parque de los Proceres (Park of the Patriots) across the street.

events: Mayaguez's festival honoring her patron saint, La Virgen de la Candelaria, around 2 Feb. each year, is among the most spectacular on the island. The annual crafts fair is held at the beginning of each Dec. at the Coliseum.

accommodations: Inexpensive hotels in town include Hotel Venezia, 62–0 Calle Mendez Vigo (tel. 833–1948); Hotel Lugo, 58 Mendez Vigo, (tel. 832–9485); and Hotel Sultana, Maquila 57. Also try the very reasonable Hotel Plata. Hotel Embajador is on 11 de Augusto Oeste. More expensive still are Parador El Sol, 9 El Sol (tel. 834–0303); La Palma (tel. 876–1446), Mendez Vigo, (834–3800); and the Mayaguez Hilton, Carr. 2, km 152.5 (tel. 834–7575, 724–0160).

food: Plenty of small, cheap lunchrooms, fast-food places, and restaurants. Vegetarians can eat at Appleseed's Restaurant near Hotel Venezia. Established eateries include the Meson Espanol, Carr. 102, km 5, and the restaurants inside the Pama, Sol, and Mayaguez Hilton.

entertainment: Pretty dull even on weekends. Best thing to do is walk around and watch the kids hanging out and trying to be cool just as they do everywhere else in the world. Check and see if Teatro Yaguez has a show on. The Mayaguez Hilton has live music nightly and dance music Tues. to Sat.

from Mayaguez: *Publicos* leaving for surrounding towns depart from the area around the plaza. If heading for Maricao, get an early start. **by air:** Eastern and American fly to San Juan's Munoz Marin International Airport. American flies to Puerto Plata, La Romana, Casa de Campo, and Santo Domingo in the Dominican Republic.

Maricao—Monte del Estado

Maricao is a small coffee-trading center near Monte del Estado, a forest preserve which, confusingly, is also called Mari-

Mountains near Maricao

cao. The preserve is one of the driest areas on the island. At the Maricao Fish Hatchery, more than 25,000 fish are reared and schooled yearly in preparation for their journey to lakes and fishponds. Open daily 8–12, 1–4:30. A trail, which begins at Km 128 on Carr 120, leads from Maricao ridge down to the hatchery.

accommodations: Apply for permission to camp at the Dept. of Natural Resources, Puerto De Tierra, San Juan, tel. 724–3724, 724–3623. Cabins at the *Centro Vacacionales* hold six and cost $20 per night. Maricao or Monte del Estado also has picnic grounds, an observation tower, and a swimming pool. Climb the stone tower for a commanding view of SW Puerto Rico. On a clear day, you can even see the cliffs on Mona Island off in the distance. More expensive is the Hacienda Juanita, Carr. 105, km 23.5. Facilities include swimming pool, tennis and other ball courts, and hiking trails.

Mona

Least known and least accessible of all Puerto Rico's offshore islands, Mona lies in the southern center of the Mona Passage. Viewed from the air, this 20-sq.-mile island appears as a per-

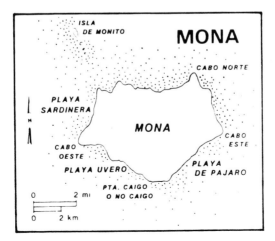

fectly flat oval surrounded by offshore coral reefs. Situated 50 miles to the W of Mayaguez, the only ways to reach it are by fishing boat from Mayaguez, private plane, or yacht. Nine miles of rough trails lead from the S shore through the dense foliage to the northern, rock-littered mesa, which gives way on three sides to a sheer 200-ft. drop to the sea below. The plateau is covered with low-lying trees and orchids, and the indigenous rock iguana (*cyclura*) scuttles furtively between rocks. Some grow as long as four feet. The only other land animals—wild boars, bulls, and goats—are descendants of livestock kept by the long-vanished pirates. The only native food is prickly pears. Water is in short supply so bring your own.

history: Mona's history is steeped in romance, much of which carries over into the present. Discovered by Columbus during his second voyage in 1493, it later became a port of call for Spanish galleons. Ponce de Leon stopped here to secure a supply of cassava bread on his way to take up his command of Puerto Rico. By 1584, most of the native Indians had been exterminated. A network of stalactite and stalagmite-filled underground caves, containing pools of spring water used to supplement the average annual rainfall of 41 inches, served as a home for pirates for nearly three centuries. Fireplaces, cooking utensils, fragments of sabers, and chains have been found inside. On the W end of the plateau are the ruins of a lodge which date from the 1930s and '40s when Mona was a popular weekend getaway for sports fishermen. Legend has it that the remains of a Spanish galleon lie just off the lighthouse and radio beacon, manned by the U.S. Coast Guard on the E end of the island.

practicalities: Camp at Playa Sardinera for $1 pp per night. Bring water and food and everything you need, *and* take it out again. For information on renting available cabins, call the Dept. of Natural Resources, tel. 722–1716.

NORTHWESTERN PUERTO RICO

RINCON

Although the name of this small town means "corner" (which suits its location perfectly), the town is actually named for Don Gonzalo Rincon, a 16th C. landowner. He granted a hill, known as *cerro do los pobres* ("hill of the poor"), to local settlers. When the town was founded years later, they named it for their benefactor. There are a half-dozen bathing beaches in this area, including Punta Higuero, where the World Surfing Championships were held in 1968. A reef to the N of town has a marina and charter boats available to take divers over to the National Wildlife Refuge surrounding Desecheo Island.

sights: Rincon's Catholic church, facing the E end of the plaza, is built on the very site which Santa Rosa de Lima, the town's patron saint, recommended when she appeared in a vision. A small chapel dedicated to her—containing plastic flowers and a model boat—stands on a ridge just beyond the intersection of Carr. 414 and Ramal 414. Pico Atalaya ("lookout peak"), easily recognizable because of its communication tower, commands a great view of the environs. A silver water tank, the sole reminder of a railroad which passed from San Juan to Ponce between 1907 and the early 1950s, stands on Cambija Street. The ruins of the storehouses and residences of the Corcega Sugar Mill (constructed 1885) remain behind trees where Corcega Beach meets Carr. 429. Rincon's lighthouse, rising 98 feet (30m) above the sea at Higuero Point, was built by the Spanish in the early 1890s. Today, the electric

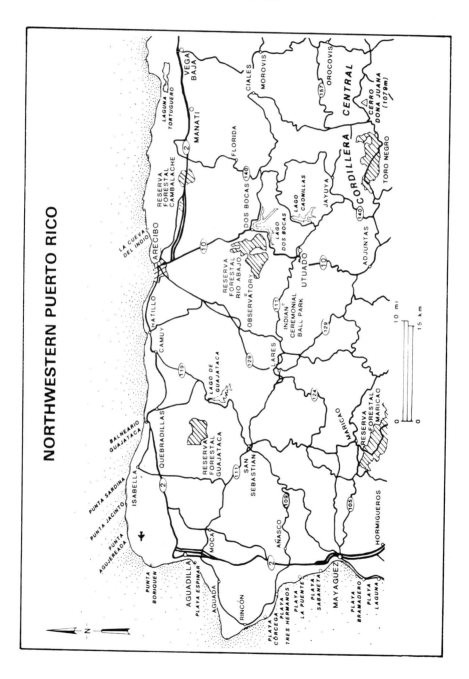

NORTHWESTERN PUERTO RICO

26,000-candlepower rotating beacon is unmanned. Down at the end of the road passing by the lighthouse are the rusting remains of the Boiling Nuclear Superheater Plant. BONUS, as it was quaintly named, was the first nuclear energy plant built in Latin America. It began operation in April 1964, but was closed down a decade later after leaks occurred.

accommodations: La Primavera is on Carr. 429. More expensive is Parador Villa Antonia at Carr. 115, km 12.3 (tel. 823–2645/2285). Villa Cofresi (tel. 823–2450, 823–2861) is at the same location. Camp at your own risk at Playa de Corcerga, Carr. 2 Salida 115.

AGUADILLA

Located on Carr 111 along the W coast, this small town boasts fine beaches, intricate lace, and fascinating historical sites. Christopher Columbus first stepped onto Puerto Rican soil somewhere between Aguadilla and Anasco on his second voyage in 1493. Since then it's undergone numerous changes! Recently the population (52,000) has declined owing to the economic depression caused by the phasing out of Ramey Air Force Base. Beaches (great snorkeling) extend from Crash Point to the north. Crash Point receives its name from the launches kept here to pick up crews in the event of a plane crash around Borinquen Point. Aguadilla is famous for its *mundillo* (finely embroidered lace) which was introduced to the area by immigrants from Belgium, Holland, and Spain. Bosque Estatal de Guajataca and Lago de Guajataca are located 30km to the E of Aguadilla.

sights: Ramey Air Force Base has been converted into Punta Borinquen, a tourist complex with complete sports facilities. Playuelas Beach is divided by what was once the pier and docking facilities for submarines and fuel tankers. Punta Borinquen Lighthouse, located W of town, has been designated a historic site worthy of preservation by the National Register of Historic Places. Severely damaged by the 1918 earthquake, this tower, built in 1870, was incorporated into

Ramey Air Force Base as a picnic area. Near the city's N entrance, between the foot of Cerro Cuesto Villa and the beach, lies the Urban Cemetery. This was established on what had once been a sugarcane hacienda. Although the 1918 earthquake destroyed many of the old tombs, those remaining are finely sculpted Italian marble. Borinquen Archaeological site, the only significant Indian site in the region, was excavated by Dr. K. G. Lathrop of Yale in the 1920s. Objects found include human skulls, shells, animal bones, and broken potsherds. Fort Concepcion is the only remaining building from the Fuerte de la Concepcion military complex which was protected by a moat, walls, and guard and sentry houses. Extensively remodeled, it now houses schoolrooms. A statue of Columbus, built in 1893, stands inside seaside Columbus Park. El Parterre Park contains *ojo de agua*, a natural spring which once served as the water supply for arriving sailors.

accommodations: Rent cabins at Punta Borinquen off Carr. 107 for $60 per night (tel. 890–6128/6330). Camp freely but

Parador Montemar, Aguadilla

NORTHWESTERN PUERTO RICO ACCOMMODATIONS

KEY: S = single, D = double; T = triple; CP = Continental Plan (Breakfast served); pw = per week; B = beach in vicinity; P = pool.

NOTE: Rates are given as a guideline only; price fluctuations can and will occur. Summer season generally runs 4/15–11/15 or 12/15; check with hotel concerned for specifics. Hotel addresses are completed with "Puerto Rico." Area code is 809. Accommodation tax of 6% applies to all listings.

ADDRESS	TELE-PHONE	WINTER			SUMMER			# OF ROOMS	NOTES
		S	D	T	S	D	T		
Parador Villa Antonio Beach Resort, Carr. 115, km 12.3, Rincon	823–2645 823–2285	37	48	53	43	53	63	53	B, P
Villa Cofresi, Carr. 115, km. 12.3, Rincon	823–2450 823–2681	75			65			75	CP, B, P
Parador Montemar, Carr. 107, km 125.4, Aguadilla	891–5959 721–2884	50	60		50	60		40	B, P
Parador Guajataca, Rte. 2, km 103.8, Quebradillas	895–3070 721–2884	52–57	55–60		52–57	55–60		38	P
Parador Vistamar, Carr. 113, km 7.9, Quebradillas	895–2065 721–2884	43	43–56		43	43–56		35	P
Parador Hacienda Gripinas, Carr. 527, km. 2.5, Jayuya	721–2884	35	40		35	40	46	19	P
Parador Casa Grande, Carr. 612, km 0, Utuado	864–3939 721–2884	45		55	45		55	20	P
Hotel Cerro Gordo, Carr. 690, km. 4, Vega Alta	883–4370	30	40		30	40		16	P
Monte Rio, H Street, Adjuntas	829–3702	25	35	40	25	35	40	23	

insecurely at Playa Crashboat, Carr. 2 Salida 458, Aguadilla. Parador Montemar (tel. 891–5959), Carr. 107, km 125.4, has rooms.

events: In honor of the world-famous composer, the Rafael Hernandez Festival is held yearly from 22 to 24 October. His music is interpreted by soloists for two days and by orchestras. Festivities surrounding the town's *fiesta patronales* go on for the two weeks around the main feast day of 4 Nov. on the main plaza. Music is performed and local specialties are cooked. Another lively time is the *Velorio de Reyes* (Three Kings Celebration). Initiated 30 years ago by a wealthy local family, a religious ceremony with music, prayers, and chants takes place on the plaza the evening of 6 January.

ARECIBO AND VICINITY

This simple but refreshing town on the Atlantic is more of a transit point or base for exploring the rest of the area than a destination in itself. The town comes alive during the annual feast of San Felipe Apostol on or around 1 May. A good jumping-off point for the beaches to the E or the mountains to the south. **getting there:** Take a *publico* from San Juan or Bayamon. Another approach would be from Ponce via Utuado, but allow for plenty of time.

sights: The town's name is derived from Aracibo, an Indian chief who had a settlement here, and a cave (La Cuevo del Indio) four miles E of town that was used for Indian ceremonies before the arrival of the Spaniards. To get here take a *publico* marked "Isolte" four km, passing along a magnificent beach. Get off at the sign and the brown cement open air igloo constructed with reinforced Coca Cola bottles. Turn right, and it's a five minute walk. Surf pounds on either side of the entrance. Descend the precipitous and makeshift staircase to view the petroglyphs adorning the walls.

accommodations and food: Highly recommended is Hotel Plaza, Ave. Jose de Diego 112 (tel. 878–2295); $8.48 s, $21.20

Near Indian Cave, Arecibo

d, $31.30 t. Campsites are at San Isidro Village, Carr. 2, km 85, Hatillo or at Punta Maracaya Camping Area, Justo Riviera, Carr. 2, km 84.6 (tel. 878–7024/2157). Plenty of cafeterias around.

Arecibo Observatory: Don't miss visiting this amazing concrete, steel, and aluminum collossus located to the S of town when tours are given on Tues. to Fri. at 2. Visitors are also admitted (no tours) on Sun. from 1–4:30 (tel. 878–2612). Reach it via Carrs. 10, 651, 635, 625; a special access road leads up to it. *Publicos* marked "Esperanza" also come here. The 600-ton platform, largest of its kind in the world, is a 20-acre dish set into a gigantic natural depression. Using this telescope, Cor-

Petroglyph, Indian Cave, Arecibo

nell University scientists monitor pulsars and quasars and probe the ionosphere, moon, and planets. Unlike other radio telescopes which have a steerable dish or reflector, the dish at Arecibo is immobile, while the receiving and transmitting equipment, which hangs 50 stories in the air, can be steered and pointed by remote control equipment on the ground. Although it costs $3.5 million annually to operate this facility, it has been responsible for several major discoveries, including detection of signals from the first pulsar and proving the existence of the quasar.

forest reserves: Lying to the E of Arecibo near Carr. 682, Cambalache Forest Reserve, a 914-acre (370-ha) subtropical forest, has 45 different species of birds. Great for hiking and picnicking. The same is true of Guajataca Forest Reserve with its limestone sinkholes and haystack hills. Sandwiched between Quebradillas to the N and San Sebastian to the S, Carr. 446 slices it in half. Cabralla, one of the longer of the 25 miles of hiking trails, ends at Lago Guajataca. Maps are available at

Arecibo Observatory

the ranger station. Camp Guajataca here may be rented on weekends when available; for information contact the Puerto Rico Council of Boy Scouts in San Juan at 767–0320. Rio Abajo State Forest is S of Arecibo. Elevations reach 1,400 feet. Here, the most rugged karst formations are found. This 5,080-acre forest was established in 1935. Although balsa, mahogany, pine and other trees are found here, it is dominated by S.E. Asian teak. A recreational center and picnic ground is open from 8 AM to 6. In all of these reserves, camping is permitted with permission obtained from the Dept. of Natural Resources in San Juan 15 days in advance.

Dos Bocas Lake: Located at km 68 on Carr. 10 at the junction of the roads to Jayuya and Utuado from Arecibo and lying parallel to Rio Abajo. Its name means "Two Mouths." This long, beautiful, and winding reservoir was created in 1942. Three launches run scheduled two-hour trips around the lake at 7, 10, 2, and 5. Although these free trips are provided as a

*Lago Dos Bocas,
Arecibo*

service for local residents, visitors are welcome to join. A one-hour trip to Barrio Don Alonso leaves daily at 12:40.

UTUADO AND VICINITY

This small, sunny mountain town is a stronghold of traditional *jibaro* culture and is one of the best places to experience Puerto Rican mountain life. You could see anything here: from a man braking his *paso fino* horse at an intersection to young *evangelisticas* "singing in the rain," holding umbrellas over megaphones and shouting the praises of the Lord Jesus. Local buses run from Jayuya, Arecibo, and up from Ponce via Adjuntas. *Publicos* also ply these routes as well as connecting with other towns in the area.

sights: Near Utuado is Caguana Indian Ceremonial Park and Museum, the most important archaeological site in the Caribbean (open daily 9-5; museum open Sat. and Sun., 10-4. To reach it, take a bus or publico ($1) or hitch 12 km E along

Ball Park, Utuado

Carr. 111 to Lares. Originally excavated by the famous archae-
ologist J. A. Mason in 1915, the park has been restored and
established under the auspices of the Institute of Puerto Rican
Culture. Don't expect much; although a loyal band keep up the
grounds, the funds needed for guides and markers have not
been supplied. The 10 *bateyes* (ball courts) are situated on a
small spur of land surrounded by fairly deep ravines on three
sides. Enter to find beautifully flowing arbors, roosters crow-
ing, and mother hens tending their chicks. The largest rectangular *bateye* measures 60 by 120 ft. (20 by 37m). Huge granite
slabs along the W wall weigh up to a ton. A few are carved
with faces (half-human, half-monkey) which are typical of
Taino-culture. One has deep, cuplike, haunting eyes. La Mujer
de Caguana, most famous of all the petroglyphs, is a woman
with frog legs and elaborate headdress. Originally, all of the
slabs were decorated with reliefs, but these have been lost due
to erosion. The *bateyes* are bordered by cobbled walkways. This
site dates from A.D. 1200. Although the ball game played in
these arenas was indigenous to the entire Caribbean, the

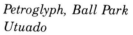
Petroglyph, Ball Park
Utuado

game reached its highest degree of sophistication in Puerto Rico. Two teams of players, thick wooden belts lashed to their waists, would hit a heavy, resilient ball—keeping it in the air without the use of hands or feet. These balls still survive in the form of stone replicas. Other examples of petroglyphs are found in Barrio Paso Palma and Salto Arriba, Utuado.

festivals and crafts: San Miguel Arcangel, the town's patron saint, has his festival on and around 29 Sept. every year. A crafts fair and Jayuya Indian Festival are held here in April. Emilio Rosado, Calle Hospital, Parcela 63, Bda. Maestro, carves masterful wooden roosters. Rafael Valentin Reyes, Barrio Judea A-Ba, Sector La Playita, makes *holajateria* (crafts from tin).

accommodations and food: Down the street from the PO and on the way to Jayuya is rundown but serviceable Hotel Vivi, operated by the former mayor of Utuado (1953–1969) Ermelindo Santiago and his son Gualberto. For those who find themselves homesick for American TV, this is the place to stay. Gualberto has installed a satellite dish and subscribes to Satellite TV Week. Also try Villas de Sotomayer (tel. 829–5015) on the way to Adjuntas. Nearest parador is *Casa Grande* on Carr. 612 at the site of a former coffee plantation. There are many places to eat in town.

FROM UTUADO

Yellow buses and publicos ply over steep hills to Jayuya, and, via Lake Dos Bocas, to Arecibo. **for Ponce:** A magnificent,

Karst landscape near Utuado

steep and cool, lushly vegetated road leads through the mountain town of Adjuntas down to Ponce and the sea below.

Jayuya: Another small mountain town with strong Indian cultural influences. Its moment in history came with the one-day "Revolution of 1950" in which *independentistas* proclaimed the Republic of Puerto Rico, burned police headquarters, and held the town for several hours before being dislodged by air assaults from the National Guard. The revolt, which was to have been coordinated with the assassination of President Truman, was quashed elsewhere before it could make much of an impact. The only industry here is Travinol, an artificial kidney factory. Jayuya's patron saint festival (Nuestra Senora de la Monserrate) takes place on and around 3 September. Held yearly in the public plaza since 1969, the Jayuya Indian festival features parades, craft markets, presentation of Taino sports and dance, plus a band which performs using indigenous musical instruments. Small carvings of faces, frogs, and spirals are inscribed on the surface of a large

Hacienda Gripinas, Jayuya

Rio Camuy Cave Park

boulder in the Saliente riverbed inside Barrio Coabey. Sol de Jayuya ("Sun of Jayuya"), found in Zama Province, is one of the most spectacular indigenous murals in Puerto Rico; it's essentially a sun equipped with eyes and mouth which reflects surprise or fear. Los Tres Picachos (3,952 ft., 1201 m), near Jayuya, is the second highest mountain in Puerto Rico. Only place to stay in town is Hacienda Gripinas, a *parador* set on the site of a 19th C. coffee plantation, $25 s, $30 d. From the *parador* climb to the top of Cerro Punta inside Toro Negro State Forest.

Parque de las Cavernas del Rio Camuy: Located on Carr. 129 at km. 19.8, Rio Camuy Cave Park (admission $4, $2.50 for children) taps the island's extensive network of underground caves. After preliminaries at the theater building, visitors take trams down into the cave entrance. Descending through 200 feet of densely foliated tropical ravine, they then proceed on foot down to the underground Camuy River—the largest underground river in the world. The upper cave, Cueva

Clara de Empalme, a dry chamber carved out by the river sometime during the past million years, is open to visitors as is the Sumidero Empalme—a 400-foot-deep, lushly vegetated pit open to the sky. Spelunkers Russell and Jane Gurnee explored and mapped the subterranean caverns in the 1950s, and they were the driving force behind the park's creation (open Wed. to Sun. from 9–5; tel. 756–5535).

Lares: *Independentista* town in the heart of coffee country where the famous Grito de Lares rebellion (see "History" under "Introduction") was raised in 1848. A white obelisk in the plaza lists the names of the revolt's heroes. Annual *independentista* rallies are still held here on 24 September in commemoration of the event. Locked amidst limestone hills, the town is cool and relaxed. Lares' *Fiesta Patronales* de San Jose, happens around 19 March.

Adjuntas: Small mountain town on the road to Ponce. Stay at Monte Rio, end of H St. (tel. 829–3708). *Fiesta Patronales* for San Joaquin and Santa Ana is held 21 August.

Puerto Rican sunset

Bosque Estatal de Toro Negro: To the E of Adjuntas en route to Barranquitas. One of the most magnificent reserves on the island (open 8–5). Also known as Dona Juana Recreation Center. Climb Cerro Dona Juana (3,341 feet, 1016 m) and Cerro de Punta, which at 4,390 ft. (1,338 m) is the tallest peak on the island. Cerro Maravilla here is the place where Puerto Rico's Watergate took place (see "recent political history" under "Government"). Hikers can also explore Inabon Falls in the heart of the reserve. Inside the reserve is a swimming pool, barbecue pits, and observation tower. Enter from Carr. 143, km 32.4.

accommodations: Camping is permitted inside the reserve if applied for 15 days in advance at the Department of Natural Resources in San Juan. Rooms are rented on a daily, weekly, or monthly basis at Quinta Dona Juana within the reserve.

Bosque Estatal de Guilarte: Divided among six areas of land and located along Carrs. 518 and 525 to the SW of Adjuntas, this reserve has Monte Guilarte, one of the few peaks on the island which remain unmarred by radio or TV towers. To the NE and lying off of Carr. 525, Charco Azul is the local swimming hole.

PUERTO RICO GLOSSARY

agregado—refers to the sugarcane workers who, up until the late 1940s, labored under the feudal system wherein wages were paid partially in goods and services received.

anatto—A small tree whose seeds, coated with orange-red dye, are used to color cooking oil commonly used in the preparation of Puerto Rican and other Caribbean cuisines.

areytos—epic songs danced to by the Tainos.

asapao—a soupy rice dish containing beef, chicken, fish, or other seafood.

bacalao—dried salt cod—once served to slaves.

barrio—a city district.

bohio—Taino Indian name for thatched houses; now applied to the houses of country dwellers in Puerto Rico.

bola, bolita—the numbers racket.

bomba—Puerto Rican musical dialogue between dancer and drummer.

botanica—stores on the Spanish speaking islands which sell spiritualist literature and paraphernalia.

calabash (calabaza)—small tree native to the Caribbean whose fruit, a gourd, has multiple uses when dried.

callejon—narrow side street; path through the cane fields.

campesino—peasant; lower class rural dweller.

canita—"the little cane," bootleg rum (also called **pitorro**).

carambola—see star apple.

Caribs—original people who colonized the islands of the Caribbean, giving the region its name.

caudillo—Spanish for military general.

cays—Indian-originated name which refers to islets in the Caribbean.

cerro—hill or mountain.

chorizo—Spanish sausage.

compadrazgo—the system of "co-parentage" which is used to strengthen social bonds in Puerto Rico.

cuerda—unit of land measure comprising 9/10ths of an acre.

cutlass—the Caribbean equivalent of the machete. Originally used by buccaneers and pirates.

duppy—ghost or spirit of the dead which is feared throughout the Caribbean. Derives from the African religious belief that a man has two souls. One ascends to heaven while the other stays around for a while or permanently. May be harnessed by good or evil through obeah. Some plants and birds are also associated with duppies.

escabeche—Spanish and Portugese method of preparing seafood.

espiritisma—spiritualism.

estadistas—Puerto Rican advocates of statehood.

Estado Libre Asociado—"Free Associated State", the Puerto Rican translation of the word commonwealth.

fiesta patronales—patron saint festivals which take place on Catholic islands.

guava—indigenous Caribbean fruit, extremely rich in vitamin C, which is eaten raw or used in making jelly.

guayacan—the tree lignum vitae and its wood.

guiro—rasp-like musical instrument of Taino Indian origin which is scratched with a stick to produce a sound.

independentistas—advocates of Puerto Rican independence.

jibaro—the now vanishing breed of impoverished but self sufficient Puerto Rican peasant.

Johnkonnu—festivities dating from the plantation era in which bands of masqueraders dressed with horse or cow heads or as kings, queens or as devils. Now a dying practice throughout the Caribbean, it is preserved largely through tourism.

langosta—spiny lobster (really a crayfish) native to the region.

lechon asado—roast pig.

machineel—small toxic tree native to the Caribbean. Its fruit, which resembles an apple, and milky sap are lethal. See clearly marked specimens near the Annaberg ruins on St. John.

mundillo—Spanish lacemaking found on Puerto Rico.

naranja—Puerto Rican sour orange; its leaves are used as medicine in rural areas.

Neoricans—term used to describe Puerto Ricans who have left for NYC and returned.

obeah—Caribbean black magic imported from Africa.

padrinos—godparents.

pasteles—steamed banana leaves stuffed with meat and other ingredients.

pastelitos—small meat-filled turnovers.

pegado—from the verb pegar (to stick together); used together with nouns in Puerto Rico as an adjective.

personalismo—used to describe the charisma of a Latin politician who appears and acts as a father figure.

pinonos—deep fried plantain rings stuffed with spiced ground beef.

plebiscite—direct vote by the people on an issue.

plena—form of Puerto Rican dance.

poinciana—beautiful tropical tree which blooms with clusters of red blossoms during the summer months. Originates in Madagascar.

publico—shared taxi found on the Spanish speaking islands.

sancocho (sancoche)—stew made with a variety of meats and vegetables; found in the Spanish speaking islands.

santos—carved representations of Catholic saints.

senorita—young unmarried female, usually used in rural Puerto Rico to refer to virgins.

star apple—large tree producing segmented pods, brown in color and sour in taste, which are a popular fresh fruit.

surrillitos—fried cornmeal-and-cheese sticks.

tachuelo—a variety of tropical hardwood.

taro—tuber also known as sasheen, tannia, malanga, elephant's ear, and yautia.

trigueno ("wheat colored")—denotes a mulatto or used to differentiate brunettes from blondes.

velorio—Catholic wake.

zemi(cemi)—idol in which the personal spirit of each Arawak or Taino Indian lived. Usually carved from stone.

BOOKLIST

TRAVEL AND DESCRIPTION

Arciniegas, German. *Caribbean: Sea of the New World.* New York: Alfred A. Knopf, 1946.

Babin, Theresa Maria. *The Puerto Rican's Spirit.* New York: Collier Books, 1971. Excellent information regarding Puerto Rican history, people, literature, and fine arts.

Blume, Helmut. (trans. Johannes Maczewski and Ann Norton) *The Caribbean Islands.* London: Longman, 1976.

Bonsal, Stephen. *The American Mediterranean.* New York: Moffat, Yard and Co., 1912.

Caabro, J. A. Suarez. *El Mar de Puerto Rico.* Rio Piedras: University of Puerto Rico Press, 1979.

Caimite. *Don't Get Hit by a Coconut.* Hicksville, NY: Exposition Press, 1979. The memoirs of an Ohio painter who escaped to the Caribbean.

Creque, Darwin D. *The U.S. Virgins and the Eastern Caribbean.* Philadelphia: Whitmore Publishing Co., 1968.

Doucet, Louis. *The Caribbean Today.* Paris: editions j.a., 1977.

Fillingham, Paul. *Pilot's Guide to the Lesser Antilles.* New York: McGraw-Hill, 1979. Invaluable for pilots.

Hanberg, Clifford A. *Puerto Rico and the Puerto Ricans.* New York: Hippocrene, 1975. Survey of the Puerto Rican historical experience.

Hart, Jeremy C. and William T. Stone. *A Cruising Guide to the Caribbean and the Bahamas.* New York: Dodd, Mead and Company, 1982. Description of planning and plying for yachties. Includes nautical maps.

Holbrook, Sabra. *The American West Indies, Puerto Rico and the Virgin Islands*. New York: Meredith Press, 1969.

Lewis, Oscar. *La Vida*. New York: Irvington, 1982. The famous (1966) chronicle of Puerto Rican life.

Lopez, Adalberto and James Petras. *Puerto Rico and the Puerto Ricans*. Cambridge, Ma.: Schenkmann-Halstead Press, 1974.

Morrison, Samuel E. *The Caribbean as Columbus Saw It*. Boston: Little Brown and Co.: 1964. Photographs and text by a leading American historian.

Naipaul, V. S. *The Middle Passage: The Caribbean Revisited*. New York: Macmillan, 1963. Another view of the West Indies by a Trinidad native.

Perl, Lila. *Puerto Rico, Island Between Two Worlds*. New York: William Morrow and Co., 1979.

Radcliffe, Virginia. *The Caribbean Heritage*. New York: Walker & Co., 1976.

Rodman, Selden. *The Caribbean*. New York: Hawthorn, 1968. Traveler's description of the Caribbean by a leading art critic.

Robinson, Kathryn. *The Other Puerto Rico*. Edison NJ: Hunter Publishing, Inc., 1988. Guide to the natural wonders of the islands.

Samoiloff, Louise C. *Portrait of Puerto Rico*. San Diego: A. S. Barnes, 1979. Descriptive and comprehensive profile.

HISTORY

Bonnet, Benitez and Juan Amedee. *Vieques En La Historia de Puerto Rico*. Puerto Rico: F. Nortiz Nieves, 1976. Traces the history of Vieques over the centuries.

Cripps, L. L. *The Spanish Caribbean: From Columbus to Castro*. Cambridge, Ma.: Schenkman, 1979. Concise history of the Spanish Caribbean from the point of view of a radical historian.

Deer, Noel. *The History of Sugar*. London: Chapman, 1950

Golding, Morton. J. *A Short History of Puerto Rico*. New York: New American Library, 1973.

Hovey, Graham and Gene Brown, eds. *Central America and the Caribbean*. New York: Arno Press, 1980. This volume of clippings from The New York Times, one of a series in its Great Contemporary Issues books, graphically displays American activities and attitudes toward the area. A goldmine of information.

Hunte, George. *The West Indian Islands*. New York: The Viking Press, 1972. Historical overview from the Western viewpoint with information added for tourists.

Knight, Franklin W. *The Caribbean*. Oxford: Oxford University Press, 1978. Thematic, anti-imperialist view of Caribbean history.

Steiner, Stan. *The Islands*. New York: Harper & Row, 1974. An in-depth living journalistic portrait of the Puerto Ricans—on their island and on the mainland *barrios*.

Van Ost, John R. and Harry Kline. *Yachtsman's Guide to the Virgin Islands and Puerto Rico*. North Miami, Florida: Tropic Isle Publishers, Inc., 1984. Where to anchor in the area.

Waggenheim, Kal. *Puerto Rico: A Profile*. New York: Praeger, 1970. A revealing if dated survey of Puerto Rico's economy, geography, and culture.

Ward, Fred. *Golden Islands of the Caribbean*. New York: Crown Publishers, 1967. A picture book for your coffee table. Beautiful historical plates.

Wood, Peter. *Caribbean Isles*. New York: Time Life Books, 1975. Includes descriptions of such places as Pico Duarte in the Dominican Republic and the Blue Mountain region of Jamaica.

FLORA AND FAUNA

Kaplan, Eugene. *A Field Guide to the Coral Reefs of the Caribbean and Florida*. Princeton, N.J.: Peterson's Guides, 1984.

Little, Elbert L., Jr., Frank J. Wadsworth, and Jose Marrero *Arboles Comunes De Puerto Rico y las Islas Virgenes*. Rio Piedras: University of Puerto Rico Press, 1967.

Riviera, Juan A. *The Amphibians of Puerto Rico*. Mayaguez: Universidad de Puerto Rico, 1978.

de Oviedo, Gonzalo Fernandez. (trans. and ed. S. A. Stroudemire. *Natural History of the West Indies*. Chapel Hill: University of North Carolina Press, 1959.

Lewis, Gordon D. *Puerto Rico: Freedom and Power in the Caribbean*. New York: Monthly Review Press, 1963. Dated but still the most comprehensive general work in existence on Puerto Rican history and economics.

Mannix, Daniel P. and Malcolm Cooley. *Black Cargoes*. New York: Viking Press, 1982. Details the saga of the slave trade.

Mendez, Eugenio Fernandez. *Historia Cultural de Puerto Rico 1493–1968*. Rio Piedras, Puerto Rico: University of Puerto Rico Press, 1980.

Silen, Juan Angel. *We, the Puerto Rican People*. New York: Monthly Review Press, 1971. Analysis of Puerto Rican history from the viewpoint of a militant Puerto Rican nationalist.

Wagenheim, Kal., ed. *Puerto Rico: A Documentary History*. New York: Praeger, 1973. History from the point of view of eyewitnesses.

Williams, Eric. *From Columbus to Castro: The History of the Caribbean*. New York: Random House, 1983. Definitive history of the Caribbean by the late Prime Minister of Trinidad and Tobago.

POLITICS AND ECONOMICS

Anderson, Robert W. *Party Politics in Puerto Rico*. Stanford, Ca.: Stanford University Press, 1965.

Barry, Tom, Beth Wood, and Deb Freusch. *The Other Side of Paradise: Foreign Control in the Caribbean*. New York: Grove Press, 1984. A brilliantly and thoughtfully written analysis of Caribbean economics.

Bayo, Armando. *Puerto Rico*. Havana: Casa de las Americas, 1966.

Blanshard, Paul. *Democracy and Empire in the Caribbean*. New York: The Macmillan Co., 1947.

Cripps, L. L. *Human Rights in a United States Colony*. Cambridge, Ma.: Schenkmann Publishing Co., 1982. Once one gets past the ludicrous paeans to life in socialist countries, this contains valuable information concerning matters one never hears about stateside: Cerro Maravilla, the Vieques and Culebra takeovers, police brutality, etc.

Diffie, Bailey W. and Justine Whitfield. *Porto Rico: A Broken Pledge*. The Vanguard Press: New York, 1931. An early study of American exploitation in Puerto Rico.

Johnson, Roberta. *Puerto Rico, Commonwealth or Colony?* New York: Praeger, 1980.

Lewis, Gordon K. *Notes on the Puerto Rican Revolution*. New York: Monthly Review Press, 1974. A Marxist analysis of the past, present, and future of Puerto Rico.

Matthews, Thomas G. and F. M. Andic, eds. *Politics and Economics in the Caribbean*. Rio Piedras: Institute of Caribbean Studies, University of Puerto Rico, 1971.

Matthews, Thomas G. *Puerto Rican Politics and the New Deal*. Miami: University of Florida Press, 1960.

Mitchell, Sir Harold. *Caribbean Patterns*. New York: John Wiley and Sons., 1972. Dated but still a masterpiece. The best reference guide for gaining an understanding of the history and current political status of nearly every island group in the Caribbean.

Petrullo, Vincenzo. *Puerto Rican Paradox*. Philadelphia: University of Pennsylvania Press, 1947.

Roosevelt, Theodore. *Colonial Policies of the United States*. Garden City, NY: Doubleday, Doran, and Co., 1937. The chapter on Puerto Rico by this ex-governor is particularly fascinating.

Tugwell, Rexford Guy. *The Stricken Land*. Garden City, NY: Doubleday & Co., 1947.

Wells, Henry. *The Modernization of Puerto Rico: A Political*

Study of Changing Values and Institutions. Cambridge, Ma.: Harvard University Press, 1969.

SOCIOLOGY AND ANTHROPOLOGY

Abrahams, Roger D. *After Africa.* New Haven: Yale University Press, 1983. Fascinating accounts of slaves and slave life in the West Indies.

Acosta-Belen, Edna and Elia Hidalgo Christensen, eds. *The Puerto Rican Woman.* New York: Praeger, 1979.

Brameld, Theodore A., *Remaking of a Culture: Life and Education in Puerto Rico.* New York: Harper & Brothers, 1959.

Horowitz, Michael H. (ed) *People and Cultures of the Caribbean.* Garden City, NY: Natural History Press for the Museum of Natural History, 1971. Sweeping compilation of social anthropological essays.

Mintz, Sidney W. *Caribbean Transformation.* Chicago: Aldine Publishing Co., 1974. Includes an essay on Puerto Rico.

Mintz, Sidney W. *Worker in the Cane: A Puerto Rican Life History.* New Haven: Yale University Press, 1960.

Price, Richard, ed. *Maroon Societies—Rebel Slave Communities in the Americas.* Garden City NY: Anchor Press, 1973.

Rand, Christopher. *The Puerto Ricans.* New York: Oxford University Press, 1958.

Steward, Julian W. *The People of Puerto Rico.* University of Illinois Press: Urbana, 1956. An early and thorough social anthropological study of Puerto Rico.

ART, ARCHITECTURE, AND ARCHAEOLOGY

Buissert, David. *Historic Architecture of the Caribbean.* London: Heinemann Educational Books, 1980.

Fernandez, Jose A. *Architecture in Puerto Rico.* New York: Hastings House, 1965.

Kaiden, Nina, Pedro John Soto, and Vladimir Andrews, eds. *Puerto Rico, The New Life.* New York: Renaissance Editions, 1966.

Rouse, Benjamin I. *Puerto Rican Prehistory.* New York: Academy of Sciences, 1952.

Willey, Gordon R. *An Introduction to American Archaeology, Vol. 2, South America.* Englewood Cliffs, NJ: Prentice-Hall, Inc., 1971.

MUSIC

Bergman, Billy. *Hot Sauces: Latin and Caribbean Pop.* New York: Quill, 1984.

LANGUAGE

Rosario, Ruben del. *Vocabulario Puertorriqueno.* Sharon, Ma.: Troutman Press, 1965. Contains exclusively Puerto Rican vocabulary.

LITERATURE

Babin, Maria Theresa. *Borinquen: An Anthology of Puerto Rican Literature.* New York: Vintage, 1974.

Baldwin, James. *If Beale Street Could Talk.* New York: Dial, 1974. Novel set in NYC and Puerto Rico.

Howes, Barbara, ed. *From the Green Antilles.* New York: Crowell, Collier, & Macmillan, 1966. Includes four stories from Puerto Rico.

Levine, Barry. *Benjy Lopez: A Picaresque Tale of Emigration and Return*. New York: Basic Books, 1980

Sanchez, Luiz R. *Macho Camacho's Beat*. New York: Pantheon, 1981. Novel set in Puerto Rico.

INDEX

SPANISH VOCABULARY

DAYS OF THE WEEK

domingo	Sunday
lunes	Monday
martes	Tuesday
miercoles	Wednesday
jueves	Thursday
viernes	Friday
sabado	Saturday

MONTHS OF THE YEAR

enero	January
febrero	February
marzo	March
abril	April
mayo	May
junio	June
julio	July
agosto	August
septiembre	September
octubre	October
noviembre	November
diciembre	December

NUMBERS

uno	one
dos	two
tres	three
cuatro	four
cinco	five
seis	six
siete	seven

ocho	eight
nueve	nine
diez	ten
once	eleven
doce	twelve
trece	thirteen
catorce	fourteen
quince	fifteen
dieciseis	sixteen
diecisiete	seventeen
dieceiocho	eighteen
diecinueve	nineteen
veinte	twenty
veintiuno	twenty-one
veintidos	twenty-two
treinta	thirty
cuarenta	forty
cincuenta	fifty
sesenta	sixty
setenta	seventy
ochenta	eighty
noventa	ninety
cien	one hundred
ciento uno	one hundred one
doscientos	two hundred
quinientos	five hundred
mil	one thousand
mil uno	one thousand one
dos mil	two thousand
un million	one million
mil milliones	one billion
primero	first
segundo	second
tercero	third
cuarto	fourth
quinto	fifth
sexto	sixth
septimo	seventh
octavo	eighth
noveno	ninth
decimo	tenth
undecimo	eleventh
duodecimo	twelfth
ultimo	last

CONVERSATION

¿Como esta usted?	How are you?
Bien, gracias, y usted?	Well, thanks, and you?
Buenos dias.	Good morning.
Buenas tardes.	Good afternoon.
Buenas noches.	Good (evening) night.
Hasta la vista.	See you again.
Hasta luego.	So long.
¡Buena suerte!	Good luck!
Adios.	Goodbye.
Mucho gusto de conocerle.	Glad to meet you.
Felicidades.	Congratulations.
Muchas felicidades.	Happy birthday.
Feliz Navidad.	Merry Christmas.
Feliz Ano Nuevo.	Happy New Year.
Gracias.	Thank you.
Por favor.	Please.
De nada.	You're welcome.
Perdoneme.	Pardon me.
¿Como se llama esto?	What do you call this?
Lo siento.	I'm sorry.
Permitame.	Permit me.
Quisiera...	I would like ...
Adelante.	Come in.
Permitame presentarle...	May I introduce ...
¿Como se llamo usted?	What is your name?
Me llamo...	My name is ...
No, se.	I don't know.
Tengo sed.	I'm thirsty.
Tengo hambre.	I'm hungry.
Soy norteamericano (-na).	I'm an American.
¿Donde puedo encontrar...?	Where can I find ...?
¿Que es esto?	What is this?
¿Habla usted ingles?	Do you speak English?
Hablo (entiendo) un poco espanol.	I speak (understand) a little Spanish.
¿Hay alguien aqui que hable ingles?	Is there someone here who can speak English?

Le entiendo.	I understand you.
No entiendo.	I don't understand.
Hable mas despacio,	Please speak more
por favor	slowly.
Repita, por favor.	Please repeat.

TELLING TIME

¿Que hora es?	What time is it?
Son las . . .	It's
. . . cinco	five o'clock
. . . ocho y diez	ten past eight
. . . seis y cuarto	a quarter past six
. . . cinco y media	half past five
. . . siete menos	five to seven
cinco	
antes de ayer	the day before
	yesterday
anoche	yesterday evening
esta manana	this morning
a mediodia	at noon
en la noche	in the evening
de noche	at night
a medianoche	at midnight
manana en la	tomorrow morning
manana	
manana en la noche	tomorrow evening
pasado manana	the day after
	tomorrow

DIRECTIONS

¿En que direccion	In which direction
queda . . . ?	is . . . ?
Lleveme a . . . , por	Please take me to . . .
favor.	
Lleveme alla, por	Please take me there.
favor.	
¿Que lugar es este?	What place is this?
¿Donde queda el	Where is the town?
pueblo?	
¿Cual es el mejor	Which is the best
camino para . . . ?	road for . . . ?
De vuelta a la	Turn to the right.
derecha.	
De vuelta a la	Turn to the left.
izquierda.	

Siga derecho. This way.
En esta direccion. In this direction.
¿A que distancia How far is it to . . . ?
  estamos de . . . ?
¿Es este el camino Is this the road to . . . ?
  a . . . ?

¿Es . . . Is it . . .
  . . . cerca? near?
  . . . lejos? far?
  . . . norte north
  . . . sur south
  . . . este east
  . . . oeste west
Indiqueme, por Please point.
  favor.

Hagame favor de Please direct me to . . .
  decirme donde
  esta . . .
  el telephono the telephone
  el excusado the toilet
  el correo the post office
  el banco the bank
  la comisaria the police station

Hundreds of other specialized travel guides and maps are available from Hunter Publishing. Among those that may interest you:

THE OTHER PUERTO RICO by Kathryn Robinson

Escaping the tourists and the crowds, this guide shows you where to find the secret beaches, unspoiled valleys, jungles and mountains of the island. Aimed at the traveller interested in outdoor adventures, each chapter explores a separate route: down the Espiritu Santo River; the Long Trails of El Yunque; beaches and birds in Guánica; tramping on Mona; scrambling through San Cristóbal; on the track of history; the heart of coffee country; Vieques by bike; and many others. Photos throughout, plus a fold-out map.
6" × 9" paperback/160 pp./$11.95

THE ADVENTURE GUIDE TO THE VIRGIN ISLANDS

by Harry S. Pariser

The most up-to-date, comprehensive, and colorful guide to both the American and British Virgins—celebrated for their incredible beauty since Columbus first discovered and named the islands in 1493. From St. Croix, St. John, and St. Thomas, to Tortola, Virgin Gorda, and Anegada, all of the islands are covered in depth. Maps of every island and town are included, with historical sections, complete sightseeing details, where to find the best food, and extensive information about hotels in all price ranges—from posh resorts to intimate guesthouses. Whether you are seeking the best walking trails at Cinnamon Bay, a good drugstore in Frederiksted, or a pay telephone on Tortola, this guide will show you the way.
5³/₈" × 8" paperback/224 pp./maps and color photos throughout/$13.95

THE ADVENTURE GUIDE TO JAMAICA

by Steve Cohen

How to explore the real Jamaica—away from the high-rise hotels—with an emphasis on walking, canoeing, cycling, and horseback riding. The best places to stay and eat, plus sections on the black market, transportation, where to shop for authentic crafts, ganja, reggae, and everything else the visitor will want to know.
5³/₈" × 8" paperback/288 pp./color photos throughout, with fold-out color map/$14.95

PUERTO RICO TRAVEL MAP

1:294,000 scale. Full color map shows all roads. Also includes maps of the Virgin Islands. On the reverse is an extensive text featuring practical information for the visitor.
Map measures approx. 2' × 3' unfolded/$7.95

THE CARIBBEAN TRAVEL MAP

Individual maps of Guadeloupe, Martinique, St. Lucia, St. Martin, St. Barts, and Dominica, plus an overall map of the islands. Full color cartography shows features of the terrain as well as all roads. Practical information for the visitor appears on the reverse.
Map measures approx. 2' × 3' unfolded/$7.95

HISPANIOLA TRAVEL MAP

1:816,000 scale color map of Haiti and the Dominican Republic. Practical travel information in the margins, plus individual town maps of Port-Au-Prince, Santo Domingo, and Cap Haitien.
Map measures approx. 2' × 3' unfolded/$7.95

MICHAEL'S GUIDES
Included in this series are volumes on:
ARGENTINA & CHILE
ECUADOR, COLOMBIA, & VENEZUELA
BRAZIL
BOLIVIA & PERU
Each is packed with practical detail and many maps. These pocket-sized paperbacks tell you where to stay, where to go, what to buy.
4¹/₄" × 8¹/₄" paperbacks/200 pp./$7.95 each

ALIVE GUIDES
BUENOS AIRES ALIVE
GUATEMALA ALIVE
RIO ALIVE
VENEZUELA ALIVE
VIRGIN ISLANDS ALIVE
Researched and written by Arnold & Harriet Greenberg, owners of the celebrated Complete Traveller bookstore in New York. These guides are the ultimate source for hotel, restaurant, and shopping information, with individual reviews for thousands of places—which to seek out and which to avoid. Sightseeing information as well.
5" × 7¹/₄" paperbacks/296 pp./$10.95 each

HILDEBRAND TRAVEL GUIDES
Among the titles in this series are:
MEXICO 368 pp./$10.95
JAMAICA 128 pp./$8.95
HISPANIOLA 143 pp./$9.95
The New York Times describes the series: "Striking color photographs, concise fact-packed writing, valuable practical information and outstanding cartography, including a fold-out map inside the rear cover."
4¹/₂" × 6³/₄" paperbacks

Plus

HUGO'S SPANISH PHRASEBOOK 128 pp. $3.25
Words and phrases are arranged by categories such as Hotels, Restaurant, Shopping, and Health. A special *menu guide* lists 600 dishes or methods of food preparation. An 1800-item *mini-dictionary* also included.

HUGO'S SPANISH IN 3 MONTHS $29.95
HUGO'S EL INGLÈS SIMPLIFICADO/ENGLISH FOR SPANISH SPEAKERS $29.95
These are intensive cassette-based courses in conversational speech. Each course comes in a vinyl album containing a 160-page book and four 1-hour cassette tapes designed to speed learning and to teach pronunciation. Together, the tapes and book take the absolute beginner to a good working knowledge of the language. The books are also available without the tapes at $5.95 each.

The above books, maps, and tape courses can be found at the best bookstores or you can order directly. Send your check (add $2.50 to cover postage and handling) to:

HUNTER PUBLISHING, INC.
300 RARITAN CENTER PARKWAY
EDISON NJ 08818

Write or call (201) 225 1900 for our free color catalog describing these and many other travel guides and maps to virtually every destination on earth.